HOW THINGS WORK

ASTONISHING
AIRCRAFT

Steve Setford

p

This is a Parragon Book
First published in 2000

Parragon
Queen Street House
4 Queen Street
Bath BA1 1HE, UK

ISBN 0-75253-673-7

Printed in Dubai, U.A.E.

Produced by
Monkey Puzzle Media Ltd
Gissing's Farm
Fressingfield
Suffolk IP21 5SH
UK

Illustrations: Alex Pang
Designer: Tim Mayer
Cover design: Victoria Webb
Editor: Linda Sonntag
Editorial assistance: Lynda Lines and Jenny Siklós
Indexer: Caroline Hamilton
Project manager: Katie Orchard

Photos by Roger Buckingham (5, 23, 27, 29, 33, 64)
and MPM Images.

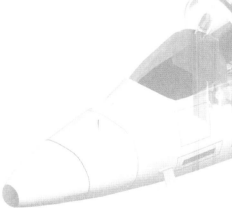

CONTENTS

FANTASTIC FLYING MACHINES

DREAMS OF FLIGHT

For thousands of years, people marvelled at the grace and ease with which birds fly through the air and dreamed of joining them. Some bold inventors made wings of feathers and leapt off high places, flapping wildly in their efforts to share the freedom of the skies. All, needless to say, failed in their attempts. Others tried to design more complicated muscle-powered flying machines. But our arms are not strong enough to keep our heavy bodies in the air. Some aviation pioneers managed to get airborne using gliders and gas-filled balloons, but they were still at the mercy of the wind. Only when people decided to use the petrol engine to power their flying machines did true flight become a reality.

Northrop Grumman A-10 Thunderbolt
Modern combat aircraft are among the most powerful weapons of war. Their guided weapons systems leave no hiding place for the enemy. One of the most fearsome is the A-10 Thunderbolt, which has a massive cannon in its nose to blast enemy tanks and artillery to pieces.

Sikorsky Sea King
Helicopters get their lift from their whirling rotor blades, allowing them to take off and land vertically, and even hover in mid-air. This makes them ideal for rescue work. Some helicopters, such as the Sikorsky Sea King, are used for rescuing people in danger at sea.

AN AIRCRAFT FOR EVERY JOB

It is about 100 years since the Wright brothers' petrol-powered *Flyer* made the first ever controlled, powered flight by an airplane. Today, there are countless different types of aircraft, from hang-gliders, helicopters and airships, to airliners, bombers and space planes. Some aircraft carry passengers and others carry cargo across the globe. Some are built for war, while others perform daring rescue missions. Some are working planes, but others exist purely for the fun of flying. This book shows you some of the most amazing planes around today, and looks at what makes them tick.

GETTING AIRBORNE

The Earth's gravity pulls all objects down towards its surface. To get off the ground, an airplane has to overcome gravity. The plane's engine provides it with thrust that drives it forwards along the runway. Air flowing over the wings produces an upward force called lift. The plane leaves the ground when the upward pull of its lift is greater than gravity's downward pull. Friction with the air creates a backward force called drag. For the plane to move forward, its thrust must be strong enough to overcome drag.

SHAPED FOR FLIGHT

An airplane's wings create lift because they have a special shape called an aerofoil. The wings have a curved upper surface, which makes air flow faster over the top than underneath. This causes a difference in air pressure that sucks the wings upwards, lifting the plane into the air. It is the force of lift that pulls the wings upwards.

Space travel
Having mastered the skies, people's attention turned to space. In 1969, the Apollo 11 astronauts became the first people to set foot on the Moon. They were launched into space by a disposable Saturn V rocket (above). Today, the reusable Space Shuttle makes regular trips into space, carrying out research and repairs to satellites.

Boeing 747
This Jumbo (below) is used to transport the Space Shuttle to the launch site. You can see the metal girders on its back to which the Shuttle is attached for flight.

CESSNA 172

Flaps
The flaps slide back and down to increase lift at slow speeds, especially when taking off and landing.

Wings
The wings produce lift. Most wings have a skin of metal panels. These are attached to a skeleton of long supports called spars, strengthened by ribs running at right angles. The place where the wing attaches to the fuselage is called the wing root.

Trailing (rear) edge of wing

Pitch

Roll

Yaw

3-D movement
The three main movements made by an airplane are called pitch, roll and yaw. Pitching is the up-and-down movement of the nose, when the plane climbs or dives. Yawing is the left-to-right movement of the nose, when the plane turns left or right. Rolling is the side to side motion, when the plane tilts or banks in a turn.

Engine
The Cessna 172 has a 160-horsepower four-cylinder engine and a top speed of 220 kph (136 mph). Most light aircraft are still powered by piston engines, in which the fuel is burnt in cylinders, driving pistons that turn the propeller. Some airplanes have turboprop engines, in which compressed air and fuel are burnt and the hot waste gases are used to turn a set of turbine blades. The turbine then drives the propeller. Many larger aircraft are powered by jet engines.

Propeller
The engine turns the propeller, which is like a set of rotating wings that pushes the air backwards and gives the plane thrust.

Wheels
The wheels and the struts that link them to the plane are called the undercarriage. The Cessna has a tricycle undercarriage, with one nose wheel and two under the fuselage.

Cockpit
This is where the pilot sits. The control column (joystick) is pushed left or right to move the ailerons, and back and forth to move the elevators. Foot pedals push the rudder left and right.

PLANE CONTROL

A car driver turns the steering wheel to go left and right. But flying a plane is rather more complicated. Not only can the plane move left and right, but it can also tip up and down and tilt from side to side. Special movable surfaces on the tail and wings, called control surfaces, change the flight path by altering the flow of air over the plane. Control surfaces include flaps, ailerons, elevators and rudders. In gliders and some light aircraft, they are moved by wires. In larger aircraft, they are moved hydraulically – that is, by the pressure of an oily fluid pumped through hollow cables. In the most sophisticated aircraft, the surfaces are controlled by computers, in a system known as 'fly-by-wire', and sometimes moved by electric motors. Most airplanes fly using a combination of several control surfaces.

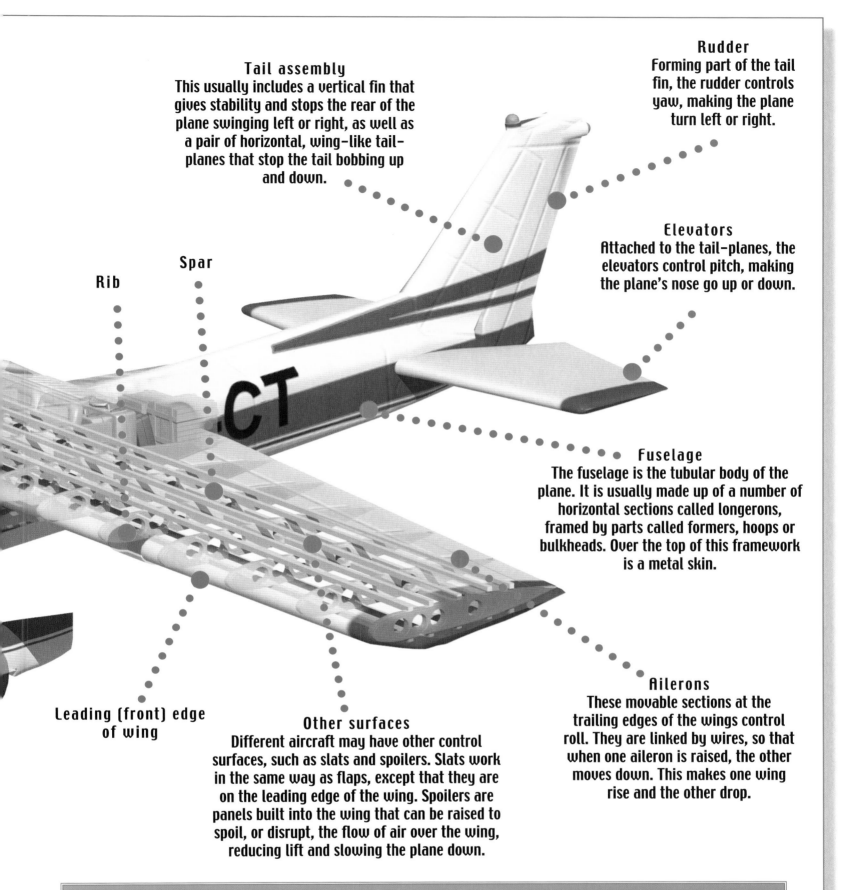

Tail assembly
This usually includes a vertical fin that gives stability and stops the rear of the plane swinging left or right, as well as a pair of horizontal, wing-like tail-planes that stop the tail bobbing up and down.

Rudder
Forming part of the tail fin, the rudder controls yaw, making the plane turn left or right.

Spar

Rib

Elevators
Attached to the tail-planes, the elevators control pitch, making the plane's nose go up or down.

Fuselage
The fuselage is the tubular body of the plane. It is usually made up of a number of horizontal sections called longerons, framed by parts called formers, hoops or bulkheads. Over the top of this framework is a metal skin.

Leading (front) edge of wing

Other surfaces
Different aircraft may have other control surfaces, such as slats and spoilers. Slats work in the same way as flaps, except that they are on the leading edge of the wing. Spoilers are panels built into the wing that can be raised to spoil, or disrupt, the flow of air over the wing, reducing lift and slowing the plane down.

Ailerons
These movable sections at the trailing edges of the wings control roll. They are linked by wires, so that when one aileron is raised, the other moves down. This makes one wing rise and the other drop.

PLANE FOR SALE

Light aircraft are small planes, usually privately owned and mainly used for leisure flying and training. Most are propeller-driven, have a single engine, and normally have a maximum of four seats. The Cessna company of the USA has been a world leader in light aircraft since World War II. Their model 150 has been used to teach more pilots to fly than any other plane in history. More than 35,000 of its descendant, the 172 Skyhawk, have been made to date. The simple, reliable and relatively cheap 172 can accommodate four people and their baggage. This all-metal plane, with its braced, high wing may look dull, but no other light aircraft can compete with it for price, comfort, range, speed and ease of operation.

WRIGHT FLYER

Propellers
The two rear-mounted wooden propellers turned in opposite directions, to make sure that the forces pushing the *Flyer* forwards were balanced. In later airplanes, these 'pusher' propellers were replaced by 'puller' propellers at the front of the plane, which were more efficient.

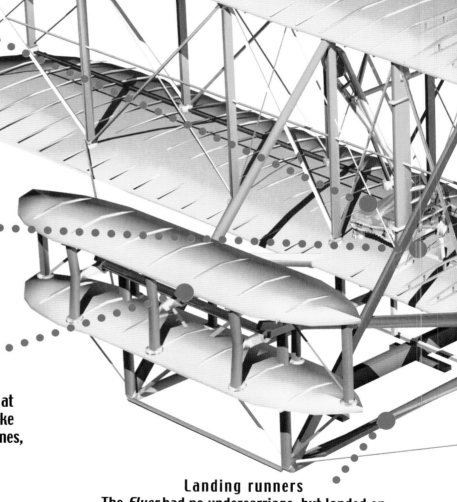

Engine
The Wrights could not find an engine light and powerful enough for the *Flyer*, so they built their own! The four-cylinder engine weighed 81 kilograms (37 pounds) and produced about 12 horsepower (an average family car engine gives about 80 horsepower).

Pilot's cradle
The pilot lay across the lower wing in a cradle positioned alongside the engine to balance its weight. Cables from the cradle controlled the rudder and wing-warping. The pilot steered by moving his body from side to side, so that the cradle pulled on the control cables.

Elevators
By adjusting the pitch of these mini-wings at the front of the airplane, the pilot could make the *Flyer* climb or descend. On modern airplanes, the elevators are usually at the rear.

Landing runners
The *Flyer* had no undercarriage, but landed on runners, which skidded across the sand.

FIRST FLYERS

On 17 December 1903, Orville and Wilbur Wright, two bicycle engineers from Dayton, Ohio, USA, launched the *Flyer* from sand dunes above the windswept beach at Kitty Hawk, North Carolina. Mounted on a small trolley and with Orville at the controls, the *Flyer's* engine kicked into life, spinning the propellers. Orville released the brake and the *Flyer* raced along the 18-metre (50-foot) take-off track, straight into the wind. There were cheers as the *Flyer* lurched up into the air. It rose to a height of about 3 metres (9 feet) and travelled for 36 metres (100 feet) before plunging down on to the sands. It was little more than a 'hop', but it marked the beginning of the age of the airplane.

WING-WARPING

For the Wright brothers getting an airplane into the sky was only half the challenge. The question remained, how do you steer it once it's airborne? The Wright brothers used a vertical rudder to make the body of the *Flyer* swing to the left or right, but to tilt the wings so that the aircraft could bank, or 'roll', in a smooth turn was more difficult. Wilbur designed a system of control wires that twisted the rear edge of the wingtips slightly when pulled. This 'wing-warping' changed the flow of air over the wings and tilted them, so that the *Flyer* could bank. Today, hinged ailerons do the same job.

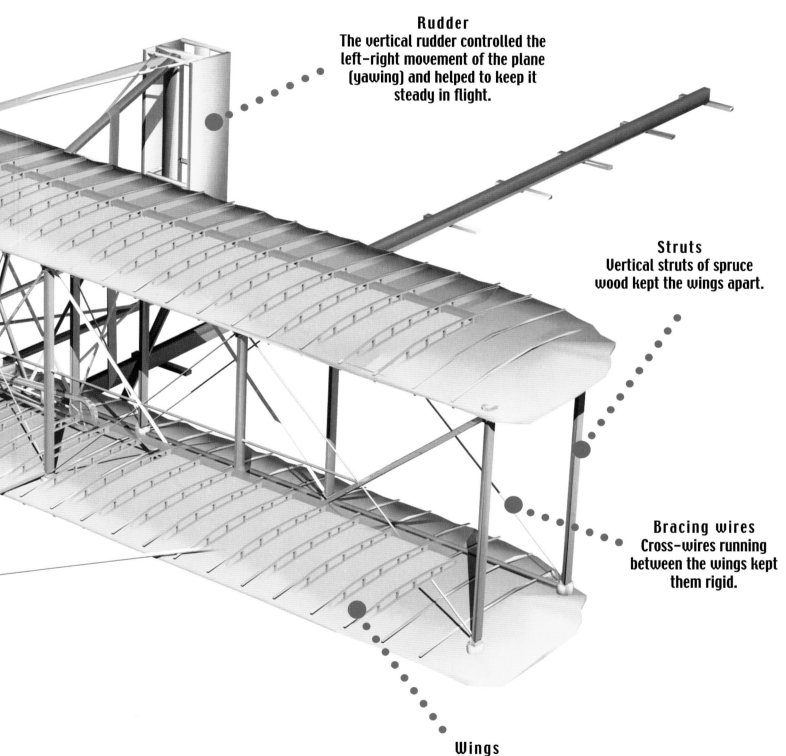

Rudder
The vertical rudder controlled the left–right movement of the plane (yawing) and helped to keep it steady in flight.

Struts
Vertical struts of spruce wood kept the wings apart.

Bracing wires
Cross-wires running between the wings kept them rigid.

Wings
The *Flyer* was a biplane, with two sets of wings, each measuring 13 metres (36 feet) long and 2 metres (6 feet) wide, covered with muslin fabric. Their wooden frame consisted of poles of spruce strengthened by cross-ribs of ash. The ribs were curved, to give the wings an aerofoil shape.

HANG-GLIDER

HITCHING A RIDE

In hitching a ride on rising thermals, hang-gliders are copying soaring birds such as eagles, condors and albatrosses. Flapping wings can be tiring work, so soaring on thermals gives the birds rest and saves energy – as well as giving them a high vantage point from which to spot prey on the ground below.

Guy lines
Steel bracing wires secure the wing and help it to keep its shape.

Battens
These rods slip into channels along the wing, stiffening it and giving it an aerofoil shape, to generate maximum lift.

Centre-line beam
This helps to balance the wing.

Body-bag
The insulated body-bag, a long fabric shell, clips to the top of the A-frame. It keeps the pilot warm and stops the pilot's legs from dangling around, giving him or her a streamlined shape.

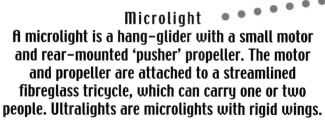

Microlight
A microlight is a hang-glider with a small motor and rear-mounted 'pusher' propeller. The motor and propeller are attached to a streamlined fibreglass tricycle, which can carry one or two people. Ultralights are microlights with rigid wings.

FLYING WING

The closest you will ever come to flying like a bird is to take to the air in a hang-glider. These kite-like craft are basically large wings, made of fabric stretched over a simple frame. There is no fuselage, so the pilot hangs underneath the wing in a special harness called a body-bag. The whole structure is so simple that it can be put together or folded away in a few minutes. When dismantled, it can easily be carried on the roof-rack of a car. Hang-gliders are leisure craft, used for racing, performing stunts or just enjoying the thrill of soaring above the ground.

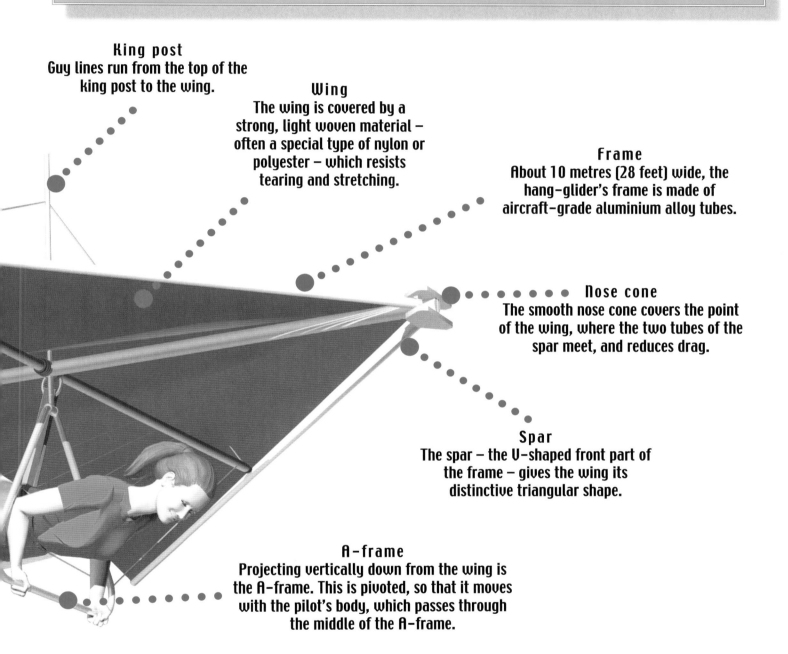

King post
Guy lines run from the top of the king post to the wing.

Wing
The wing is covered by a strong, light woven material – often a special type of nylon or polyester – which resists tearing and stretching.

Frame
About 10 metres (28 feet) wide, the hang-glider's frame is made of aircraft-grade aluminium alloy tubes.

Nose cone
The smooth nose cone covers the point of the wing, where the two tubes of the spar meet, and reduces drag.

Spar
The spar – the V-shaped front part of the frame – gives the wing its distinctive triangular shape.

A-frame
Projecting vertically down from the wing is the A-frame. This is pivoted, so that it moves with the pilot's body, which passes through the middle of the A-frame.

KEEPING CONTROL

To launch a hang-glider, the pilot runs into the wind from the top of a steep hill and is lifted by the wing. There are no rudders, ailerons or elevators, so the pilot holds the control bar and steers by moving his or her body, which in turn moves the wing. Pushing the bar forward makes the hang-glider climb, pulling on it makes it descend. Turns are made by shifting the body from side to side.

Experienced pilots soar on currents of rising warm air called thermals. To cover long distances, the pilot makes the hang-glider climb on one thermal, then glides down and rises again on the next thermal, and so on. By hitching rides on thermals, a hang-glider can stay airborne for more than two hours and travel over 150 kilometres (90 miles).

MOTORIZED GLIDER

Power plant
The 54-horsepower, two-stroke engine and propeller, weighing less than 50 kilograms (23 pounds), are raised for take-off but then retracted back into the fuselage. In flight, doors close over the engine housing to keep the fuselage streamlined.

Materials
Modern gliders are made out of tough, lightweight materials such as fibreglass, carbon-fibre and kevlar. Older gliders were either wood or metal.

Canopy
The cockpit canopy, made of clear plastic such as perspex, gives an excellent all-round view. To get in and out, the pilot lifts up the canopy, which is hinged at the front end.

Nose tow hole
The towing cable attaches here.

Cockpit
This glider has a single seat. Training gliders have more bulging canopies, two seats and dual controls, so the instructor can take over the flight if necessary.

Seat
The semi-reclining seat keeps the pilot's body low in the cockpit, allowing the canopy to follow the smooth lines of the fuselage.

RIDING AIR CURRENTS
A glider cannot glide upwards, or even maintain level flight, so the pilot keeps the nose pointed just below the horizon and glides downwards. But the plane can still climb, even in this downward-pointing position, by soaring on air currents that rise faster than the plane sinks. These air currents include thermals and slope winds (winds deflected upwards by a hillside), and they allow a glider to stay aloft for many hours.

Main wheel
The glider has a single, retractable wheel under the fuselage. Having just one wheel means that when it is at rest, one wing touches the ground, so a helper is needed to hold up the wing during the first part of the take-off. There may be a small wheel or skid under the tail to prevent damage on landing. Some gliders also have a nose wheel.

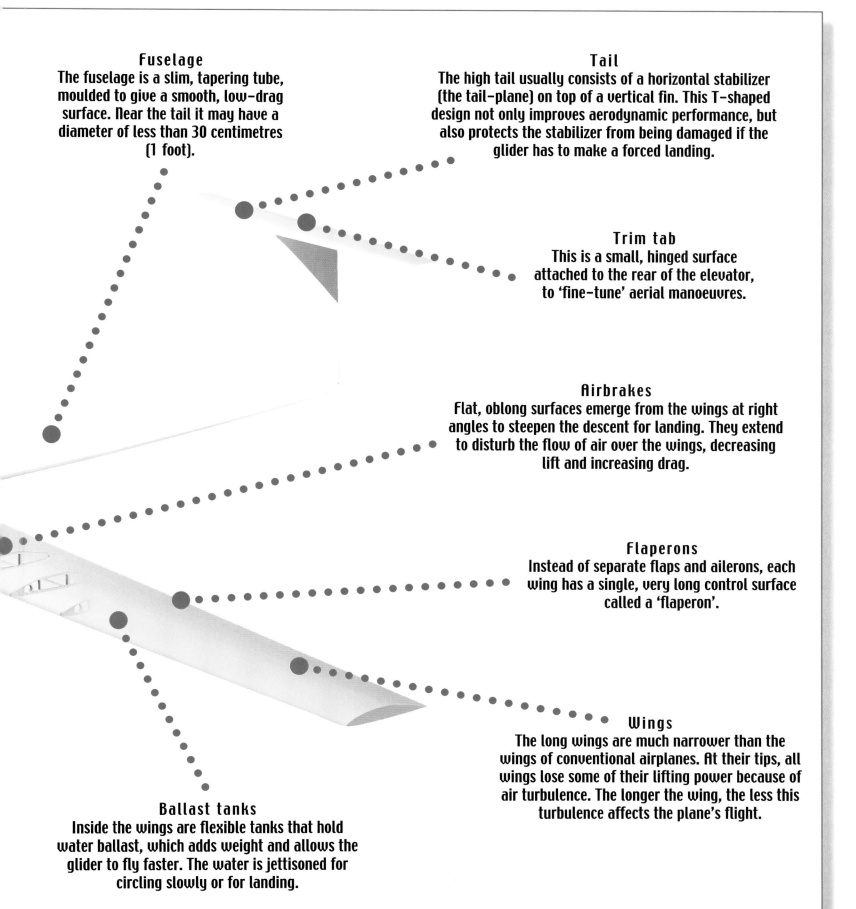

Fuselage
The fuselage is a slim, tapering tube, moulded to give a smooth, low-drag surface. Near the tail it may have a diameter of less than 30 centimetres (1 foot).

Tail
The high tail usually consists of a horizontal stabilizer (the tail-plane) on top of a vertical fin. This T-shaped design not only improves aerodynamic performance, but also protects the stabilizer from being damaged if the glider has to make a forced landing.

Trim tab
This is a small, hinged surface attached to the rear of the elevator, to 'fine-tune' aerial manoeuvres.

Airbrakes
Flat, oblong surfaces emerge from the wings at right angles to steepen the descent for landing. They extend to disturb the flow of air over the wings, decreasing lift and increasing drag.

Flaperons
Instead of separate flaps and ailerons, each wing has a single, very long control surface called a 'flaperon'.

Wings
The long wings are much narrower than the wings of conventional airplanes. At their tips, all wings lose some of their lifting power because of air turbulence. The longer the wing, the less this turbulence affects the plane's flight.

Ballast tanks
Inside the wings are flexible tanks that hold water ballast, which adds weight and allows the glider to fly faster. The water is jettisoned for circling slowly or for landing.

GETTING AIRBORNE
Being engine-less airplanes, gliders need help to get them moving so that the air flowing over the wings generates enough lift for take-off. Gliders may be launched by being towed into the air by a light airplane called a 'tug'. The glider is tied to the plane by a long cable, which the pilot releases at the desired height by pulling a knob in the cockpit. A winch-launch uses a powerful winch to pull the glider along. The cable, up to 2 kilometres (1.25 miles) long, may have a small parachute to slow its descent after release. In an auto-tow, a car tows the glider along like a kite until it gets airborne. Motorized gliders have retractable engines that are used only for take-off and in emergencies.

BREITLING ORBITER 3

Burners
The six burners, separated from the capsule by a protective heat shield, generated hot air.

Gas valves
If the pilots wanted to level off or descend, they expelled helium through valves in the top of the gas tanks.

Stores of food, water, and emergency equipment

Cockpit
Using switches on the cockpit's instrument panel, the pilots could operate the burners, change fuel tanks and jettison empty tanks from inside the capsule. For communicating with their base in Geneva, Switzerland, and air-traffic control centres around the world the cockpit was equipped with satellite telephone, radios and a laptop computer to send faxes.

Capsule details
The cramped capsule was made of kevlar (a super-tough plastic) and carbon-fibre. It was well insulated to protect the pilots from the freezing outside temperatures, which sometimes plummeted to −58 ° C. The capsule included sleeping quarters, food and water stores, a toilet and mini-kitchen, oxygen for breathing, and an air-filtering system.

LIGHTER-THAN-AIR CRAFT

The first ever sustained flight was made in 1783 by the French Montgolfier brothers' hot-air balloon. The balloon's envelope was made of paper and hot air was produced by burning straw.

Balloons are basically bags or 'envelopes' of hot air or gas such as hydrogen or helium. In a hot-air balloon, burners heat the air inside the envelope. The air expands as it is heated, which makes it lighter than the air outside and gives the balloon lift. A gas balloon contains gas that is naturally lighter (less dense) than air, so it floats in the atmosphere. Hot-air balloons burn propane or kerosene for fuel. Today, scientists use balloons to carry instruments that gather information about the weather. Other balloons, used for racing and leisure trips, have a basket attached beneath the envelope to carry passengers.

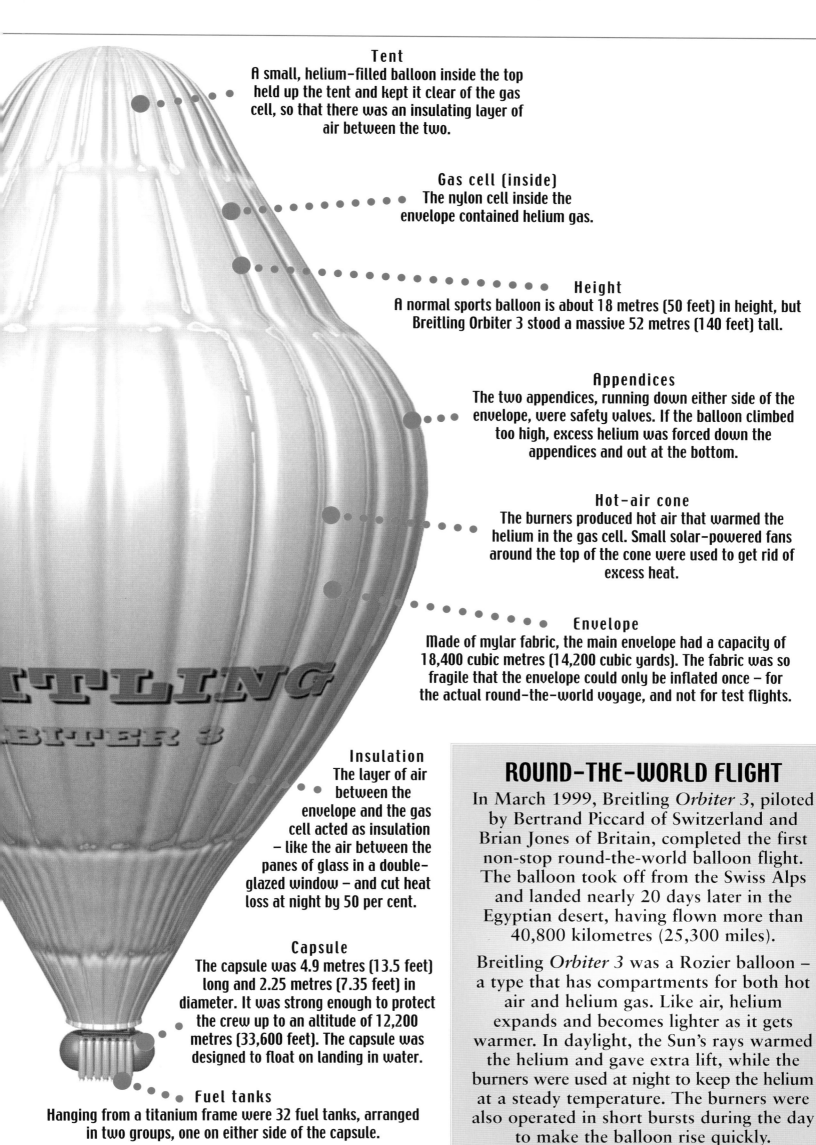

Tent
A small, helium-filled balloon inside the top held up the tent and kept it clear of the gas cell, so that there was an insulating layer of air between the two.

Gas cell (inside)
The nylon cell inside the envelope contained helium gas.

Height
A normal sports balloon is about 18 metres (50 feet) in height, but Breitling Orbiter 3 stood a massive 52 metres (140 feet) tall.

Appendices
The two appendices, running down either side of the envelope, were safety valves. If the balloon climbed too high, excess helium was forced down the appendices and out at the bottom.

Hot-air cone
The burners produced hot air that warmed the helium in the gas cell. Small solar-powered fans around the top of the cone were used to get rid of excess heat.

Envelope
Made of mylar fabric, the main envelope had a capacity of 18,400 cubic metres (14,200 cubic yards). The fabric was so fragile that the envelope could only be inflated once – for the actual round-the-world voyage, and not for test flights.

Insulation
The layer of air between the envelope and the gas cell acted as insulation – like the air between the panes of glass in a double-glazed window – and cut heat loss at night by 50 per cent.

Capsule
The capsule was 4.9 metres (13.5 feet) long and 2.25 metres (7.35 feet) in diameter. It was strong enough to protect the crew up to an altitude of 12,200 metres (33,600 feet). The capsule was designed to float on landing in water.

Fuel tanks
Hanging from a titanium frame were 32 fuel tanks, arranged in two groups, one on either side of the capsule.

ROUND-THE-WORLD FLIGHT

In March 1999, Breitling *Orbiter 3*, piloted by Bertrand Piccard of Switzerland and Brian Jones of Britain, completed the first non-stop round-the-world balloon flight. The balloon took off from the Swiss Alps and landed nearly 20 days later in the Egyptian desert, having flown more than 40,800 kilometres (25,300 miles).

Breitling *Orbiter 3* was a Rozier balloon – a type that has compartments for both hot air and helium gas. Like air, helium expands and becomes lighter as it gets warmer. In daylight, the Sun's rays warmed the helium and gave extra lift, while the burners were used at night to keep the helium at a steady temperature. The burners were also operated in short bursts during the day to make the balloon rise quickly.

HINDENBURG AIRSHIP

Gas bags
The *Hindenburg* contained 16 air-tight gas bags, made from 1.5 million ox bladders. Wire mesh separated them from the outer fabric and metal framework. The gas bags contained nearly 200,000 cubic metres of highly inflammable hydrogen gas, which made the airship lighter than the air around it and gave it lift.

Framework
The spindly framework, made of a strong aluminium alloy called duralumin, consisted of a series of vertical hoops linked by ribs running crossways and strengthened by bracing wires.

Outer fabric
The outer fabric was cotton, specially treated so that it was airtight and reinforced where it stretched over the metal framework. Minor tears could be repaired in the air by lowering engineers down the sides of the ship on ropes.

Fuel and water tanks
The fuel tanks could carry enough diesel for a trip of more than 17,000 kilometres (10,550 miles). As well as water for the passengers and crew, the water tanks also held water as ballast. To take off, some ballast was released and the airship rose.

Control gondola
The nerve centre of the *Hindenburg* was the small control car, where officers kept the airship on course.

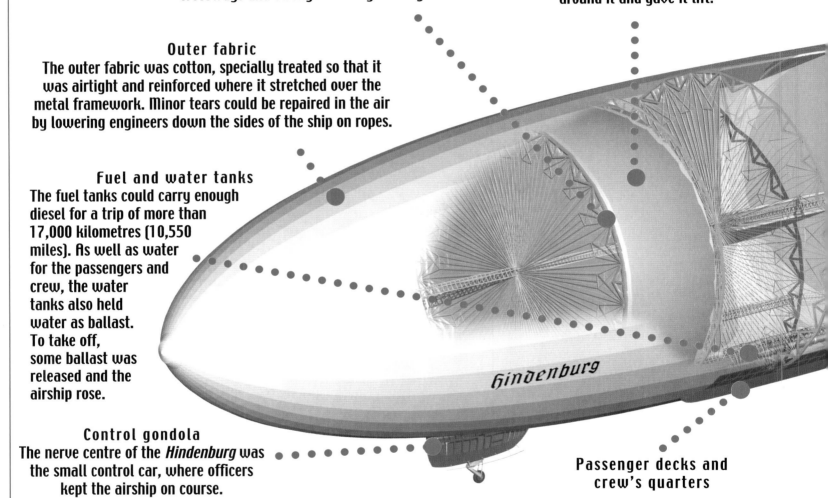

Passenger decks and crew's quarters

THE AIRSHIP AGE

Airships are lighter-than-air craft which have engines and steering mechanisms. Early airships, built in the late nineteenth century, were cloth-covered, cigar-shaped gas bags, which kept their shape because the gas inside was under high pressure. If the bag sprung a leak, the shape was lost and the airship became difficult to control. So a new type of airship, the 'rigid' was developed, with a strong internal framework made of lightweight metal alloys.

Rigid airships were used in World War I for reconnaissance missions and bombing raids. After the war, they were used to carry passengers on long-distance journeys. In the mid-1930s, airships established the first regular transatlantic air services. Airship travel was expensive and only a small number of passengers could be carried at a time. But airships crossed the Atlantic twice as quickly as the great ocean liners, and the passengers enjoyed an equal level of comfort.

MONSTER OF THE SKIES

Measuring 245 metres (670 feet) long – three times the length of a modern jumbo jet – the German airship *Hindenburg* was the largest craft ever to take to the skies. On a 50–65-hour transatlantic trip it could carry up to 50 passengers in spacious and luxurious accommodation. The crew usually numbered between 50–60, including 10–15 stewards to look after the passengers' needs.

The *Hindenburg* flew for the first time in 1936, and made 18 successful transatlantic trips in all. It took off on its last voyage from Frankfurt, Germany, on 3 May 1937. Disaster struck when it arrived at Lakehurst, New Jersey, USA, on 6 May. Suddenly, the *Hindenburg* caught fire and exploded in a ball of flame, killing 35 of the 97 people on board. The tragedy signalled the end of the airship age, and these vast giants of the skies were soon replaced on transatlantic voyages by flying-boat airplanes.

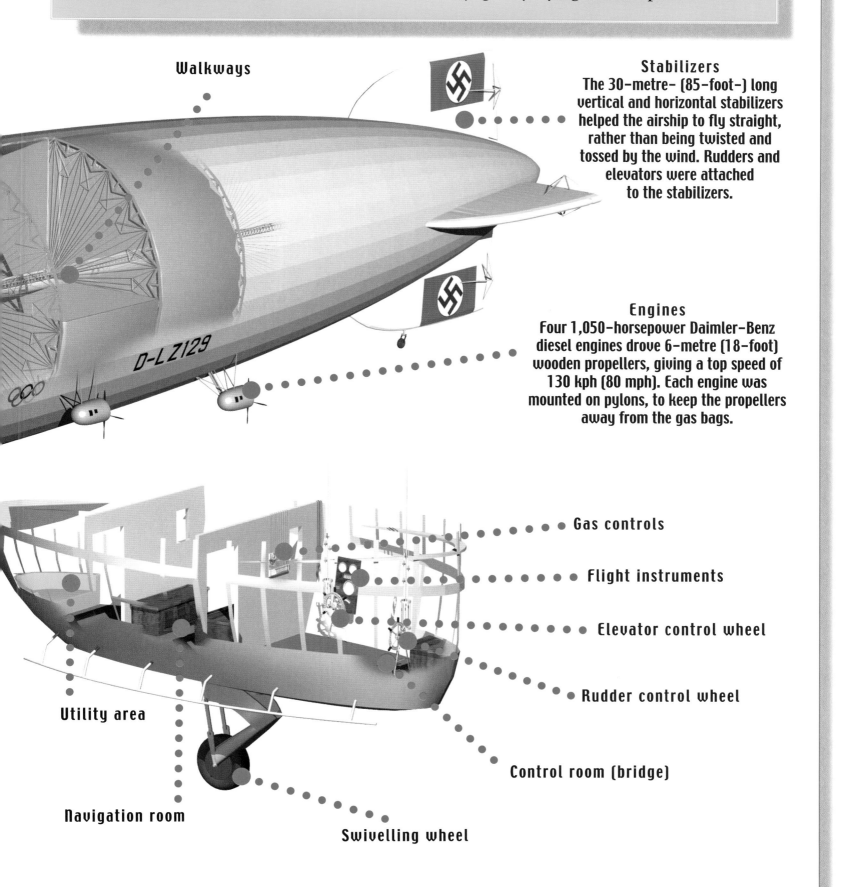

Walkways

Stabilizers
The 30-metre- (85-foot-) long vertical and horizontal stabilizers helped the airship to fly straight, rather than being twisted and tossed by the wind. Rudders and elevators were attached to the stabilizers.

Engines
Four 1,050-horsepower Daimler-Benz diesel engines drove 6-metre (18-foot) wooden propellers, giving a top speed of 130 kph (80 mph). Each engine was mounted on pylons, to keep the propellers away from the gas bags.

D-LZ129

Gas controls

Flight instruments

Elevator control wheel

Rudder control wheel

Control room (bridge)

Utility area

Navigation room

Swivelling wheel

FOKKER DR.I TRIPLANE

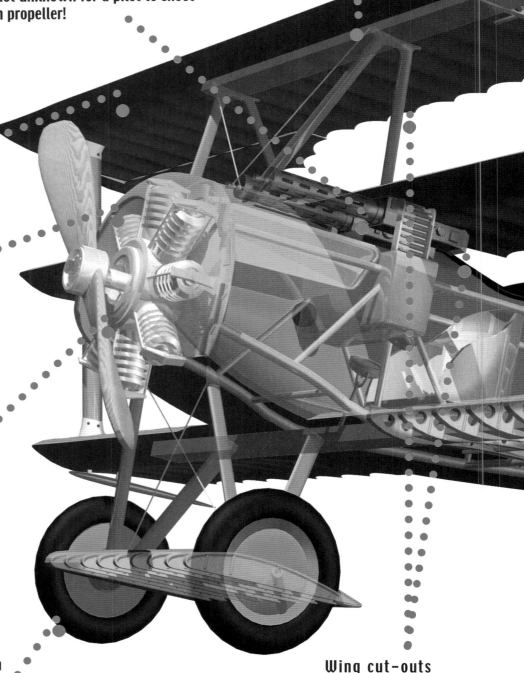

Guns
The Fokker had two fixed, forward-firing Spandau machine guns mounted above the engine. World War I fighters used a timing device called an interrupter, which allowed the guns to fire between the spinning propeller blades. However, interrupters were not fail-safe, and it was not unknown for a pilot to shoot off his own propeller!

Wing-span
The span of the longest wing set – the upper one – was only just over 7 metres (20 feet). Having three tiers of short wings made the Fokker DR.I very manoeuvrable in aerial battles.

Wings
The Fokker DR.I had three sets of wings of different sizes, with the upper set being the longest and the lower set the shortest. The wings were made of fabric over a plywood frame.

Engine cowling
This metal cover prevented the pilot and plane from getting covered with oil thrown out by the engine.

Engine
The DR.I's power plant was a 110-horsepower Oberursel UR II or Le Rhone nine-cylinder rotary engine. The cylinders were arranged in a ring and rotated with the propeller around a stationary crank shaft. The engine was started by a mechanic on the ground spinning the propeller.

Undercarriage
The two landing wheels were mounted on rigid struts. Unlike the wheels of most modern planes, they could not be withdrawn into the fuselage after take-off.

Wing cut-outs
To improve the pilot's view from the cockpit, curves were cut out of the upper and middle wings.

THREE-WINGED FIGHTER

Germany's Fokker DR.I triplane entered service in 1917, and for a while it proved unbeatable. The DR.I had three sets of wings, while most other fighters of the time were biplanes or monoplanes. Although its top speed was slower than other fighters', the DR.I could climb quicker and was unmatched in manoeuvrability – two qualities that gave it a crucial advantage in tight dog-fights.

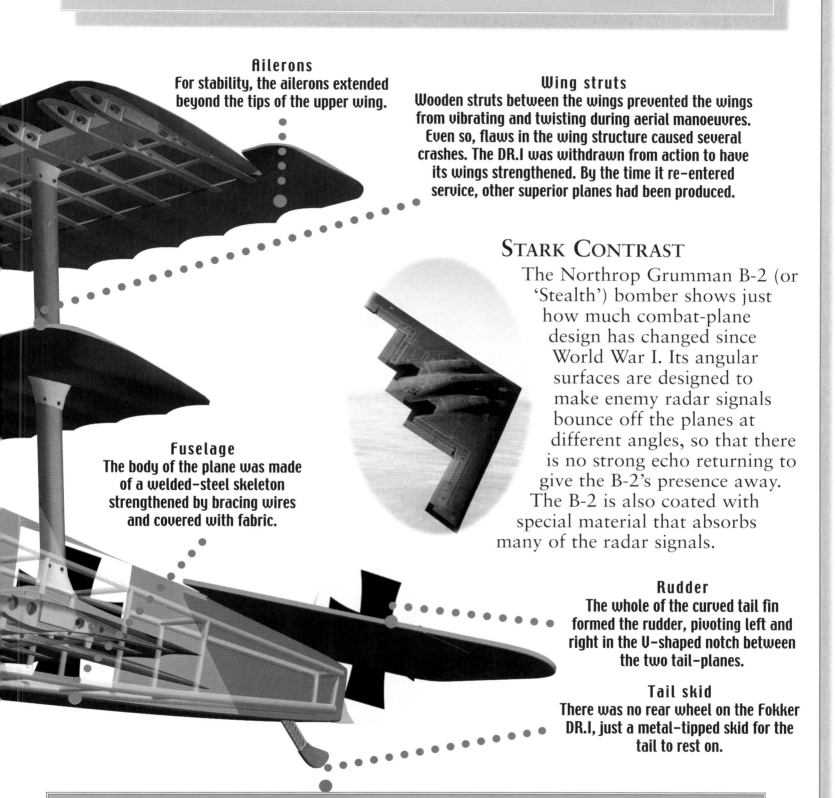

Ailerons
For stability, the ailerons extended beyond the tips of the upper wing.

Wing struts
Wooden struts between the wings prevented the wings from vibrating and twisting during aerial manoeuvres. Even so, flaws in the wing structure caused several crashes. The DR.I was withdrawn from action to have its wings strengthened. By the time it re-entered service, other superior planes had been produced.

STARK CONTRAST

The Northrop Grumman B-2 (or 'Stealth') bomber shows just how much combat-plane design has changed since World War I. Its angular surfaces are designed to make enemy radar signals bounce off the planes at different angles, so that there is no strong echo returning to give the B-2's presence away. The B-2 is also coated with special material that absorbs many of the radar signals.

Fuselage
The body of the plane was made of a welded-steel skeleton strengthened by bracing wires and covered with fabric.

Rudder
The whole of the curved tail fin formed the rudder, pivoting left and right in the U-shaped notch between the two tail-planes.

Tail skid
There was no rear wheel on the Fokker DR.I, just a metal-tipped skid for the tail to rest on.

THE RED BARON

The German flyer Manfred von Richtofen was the most successful fighter pilot of World War I, shooting down a total of 80 aircraft. He was known as the Red Baron, because of the bright red Fokker DR.I triplane he flew. Von Richtofen's squadron, all in brightly coloured DR.Is to startle the enemy, ruled the skies and were nicknamed the 'Flying Circus' by Allied pilots. Von Richtofen was killed on 21 April 1918, when his triplane crashed to the ground after being attacked simultaneously by anti-aircraft guns and a Sopwith Camel fighter flown by Canadian pilot Roy Brown.

SPIRIT OF ST LOUIS

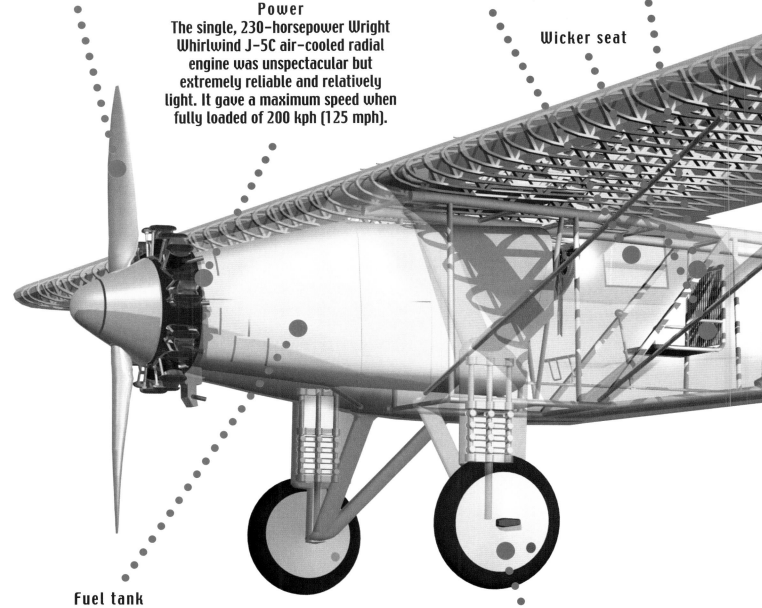

Cockpit
To accommodate the fuel tank, the cockpit had to be moved further back along the fuselage than normal.

Windows
There were only two small side windows, one on either side of the cockpit. When he felt drowsy, Lindbergh would open a window to get a blast of icy air to wake himself up.

Propeller
The 2.7-metre- (7.4-foot-) diameter propeller had two blades made of duralumin – a strong, lightweight aluminium alloy.

Power
The single, 230-horsepower Wright Whirlwind J-5C air-cooled radial engine was unspectacular but extremely reliable and relatively light. It gave a maximum speed when fully loaded of 200 kph (125 mph).

Wicker seat

Fuel tank
The huge fuel tank, immediately behind the engine, blocked direct forward vision. It could hold 1,700 litres (121 gallons) and gave the plane an astonishing range of 6,600 kilometres (4,090 miles).

Undercarriage
The two fixed, spoked wheels were covered with cotton to make them more streamlined.

LEGENDARY AIRCRAFT

In 1927, this single-engine monoplane carried American Charles Lindbergh on the first solo non-stop flight across the Atlantic. Funded by a group of businessmen, Lindbergh asked the Ryan company of San Diego to build him a plane that would win the US$25,000 prize offered to the first pilot who could fly the Atlantic single-handed. The *Spirit of St Louis* was based on Ryan's standard M-1 five-passenger aircraft, modified to Lindbergh's specifications. The plane was stripped down to the bare essentials, so that it could carry as much fuel as possible.

Already tired from a sleepless night, Lindbergh took off from the muddy Roosevelt airfield, New York, at 7.54 am on 20 May...

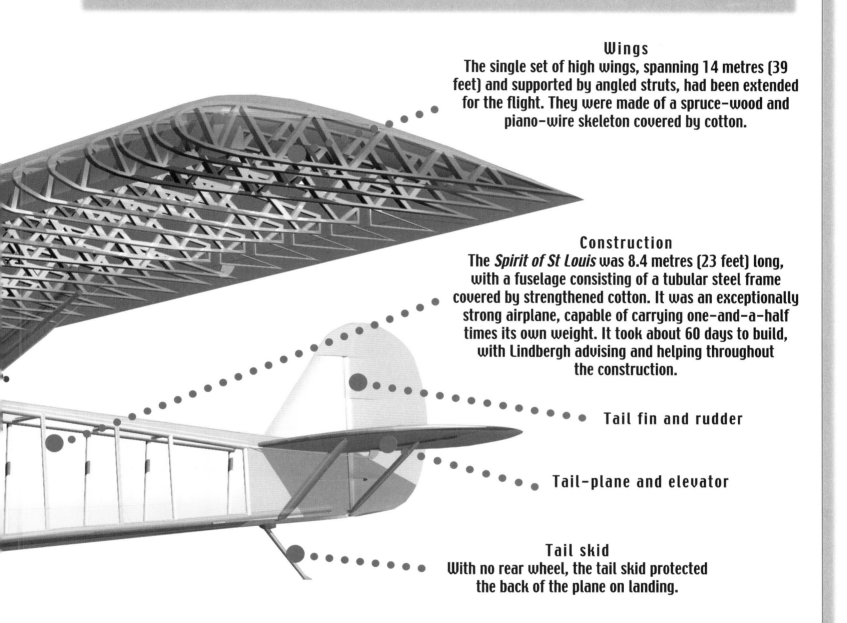

Wings
The single set of high wings, spanning 14 metres (39 feet) and supported by angled struts, had been extended for the flight. They were made of a spruce-wood and piano-wire skeleton covered by cotton.

Construction
The *Spirit of St Louis* was 8.4 metres (23 feet) long, with a fuselage consisting of a tubular steel frame covered by strengthened cotton. It was an exceptionally strong airplane, capable of carrying one-and-a-half times its own weight. It took about 60 days to build, with Lindbergh advising and helping throughout the construction.

Tail fin and rudder

Tail-plane and elevator

Tail skid
With no rear wheel, the tail skid protected the back of the plane on landing.

GRUELLING VOYAGE

The *Spirit of St Louis* was not easy to fly, as it was nose-heavy when fully loaded, and the wings lost much of their efficiency in turbulent air. It had only basic navigation equipment and flight instruments. Fortunately, Lindbergh was skilled and experienced in the air, having flown with the US Army before becoming a stunt flyer and then a long-distance airmail pilot.

Lindbergh finally reached Paris, France, at 10.24 pm on 21 May, after 33 hours and 30 minutes in the air – and 150,000 people at Le Bourget airfield welcomed him as a hero.

GEE BEE R-2 SUPER SPORTSTER

Fuselage
The fuselage, made of metal and wood, was only 5.4 metres (15 feet) long.

Balancing act
To balance the engine's weight, the pilot and cockpit had to be at the other end of the plane, tucked at the base of the short tail fin.

Flying engine
The R-2 had a 535-horsepower Pratt and Witney R985 engine stuffed into its nose, giving it a top speed of 413 kph (256 mph). The R-1 had a larger 800-horsepower Pratt and Witney R1340 Wasp engine.

Performance
The Super Sportsters performed superbly in knife-edge turns (with the plane tipped on its side) and even upside down. But landing and looping manoeuvres were a little hair-raising for the pilots.

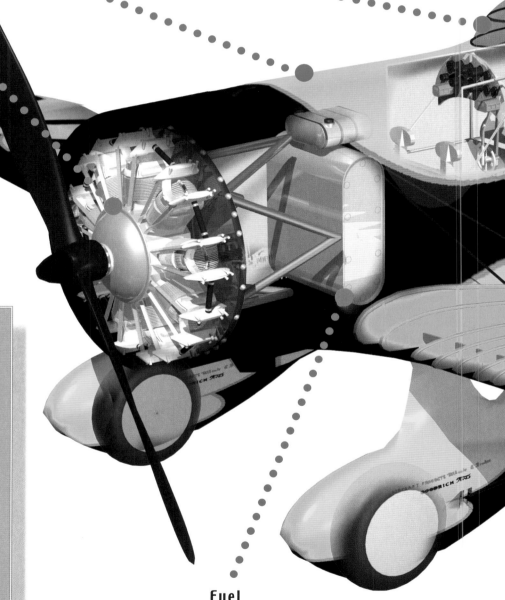

FLYING FOR FUN

After the end of World War I, many pilots turned their flying skills to entertaining the public at airshows. During the 1920s air races were all the rage, with daredevil pilots risking all for big-money prizes. A new breed of airplane emerged, designed purely for speed. Ever larger engines were crammed into smaller and smaller fuselages.

Among the most famous race planes were America's Gee Bee Super Sportsters, built by Granville Brothers of Springfield, Massachusetts. The four brothers began making two-seat biplanes for private use, but then switched to racers. The most famous of these were the R-1 and R-2 Super Sportsters.

Fuel
The tank held about 1,150 litres (82 gallons) of fuel, compared to the 605 litres (43 gallons) carried by the R-1.

POWERFUL BUT DANGEROUS

The R-1 was little more than an enormous engine bolted on to a tiny body. In 1932, Major James Doolittle piloted the R-1 to victory in the Thompson Trophy race, flying laps around a circuit marked out by pylons. The R-1's sister plane, the R-2, looked almost identical. It had a slightly less powerful but more fuel-efficient engine than the R-1 and a larger fuel tank, allowing it to fly long-distance races with fewer refuelling stops. This gave it a better average speed.

All the Granville Brothers' racers were successful, but only the most skilled flyers could handle them. Over the space of four years, seven Gee Bee racers crashed, killing five pilots, leading to the company ceasing production.

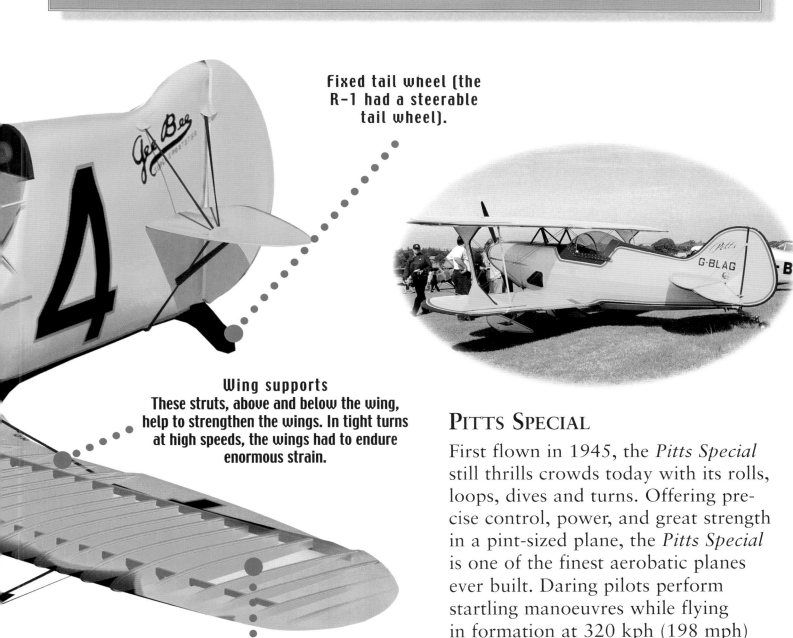

Fixed tail wheel (the R-1 had a steerable tail wheel).

Wing supports
These struts, above and below the wing, help to strengthen the wings. In tight turns at high speeds, the wings had to endure enormous strain.

Clipped wings
The R-2's wing-span was just 7.6 metres (21 feet).

PITTS SPECIAL

First flown in 1945, the *Pitts Special* still thrills crowds today with its rolls, loops, dives and turns. Offering precise control, power, and great strength in a pint-sized plane, the *Pitts Special* is one of the finest aerobatic planes ever built. Daring pilots perform startling manoeuvres while flying in formation at 320 kph (198 mph) with the wing-tips often no more than 3 metres (8 feet) apart!

FATAL FLIGHTS

The planes were said to be dangerous – and they were. Both the R-1 and R-2 crashed in 1933. The parts were salvaged and reused in the form of the R-1/R-2, which had a larger fuel tank set further back than before. This upset the plane's balance, making it impossible to control – it crashed on its first flight killing its pilot, Allen Granville.

BOEING 314 CLIPPER

Navigation dome
To check the plane was on course on long ocean flights, where there were no familiar landmarks or coastlines, navigators would look out of this dome and note the positions of stars.

Upper deck
This contained the flight deck, the crew's quarters, and compartments for cargo and the passengers' luggage.

Baggage compartment

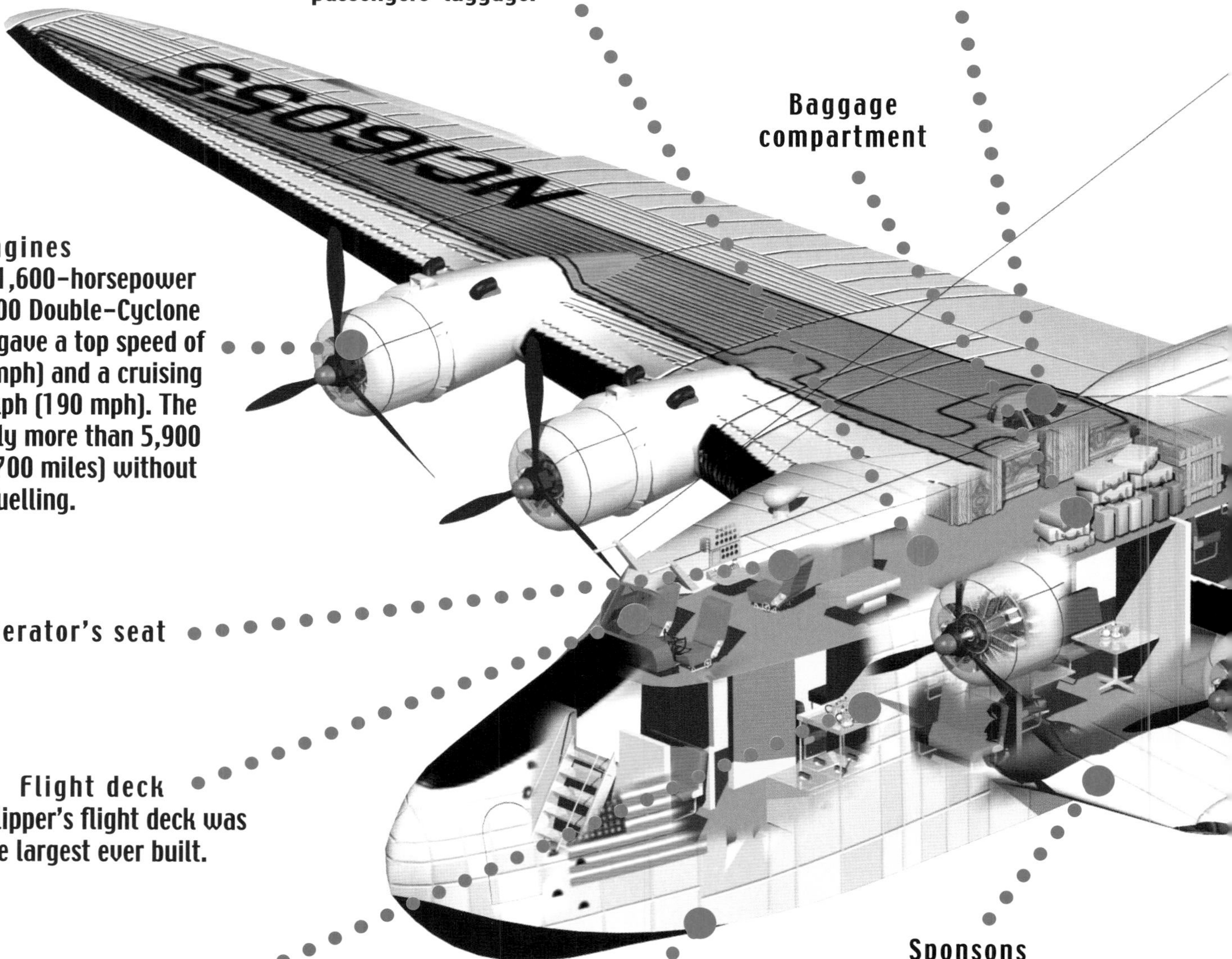

Engines
Four massive 1,600-horsepower Wright GR-2600 Double-Cyclone radial engines gave a top speed of 340 kph (210 mph) and a cruising speed of 302 kph (190 mph). The Clipper could fly more than 5,900 kilometres (3,700 miles) without refuelling.

Radio operator's seat

Flight deck
The Clipper's flight deck was the largest ever built.

Galley (kitchen)
The in-flight food was of the highest order. Chefs recruited from top hotels oversaw preparation at the flying boat terminal and the meals were cooked in the galley during the flight. At mealtimes, the tables were set with fine china and silver cutlery. Two waiters served the hungry diners.

Fuselage
The all-metal fuselage, nearly 6 metres (9 feet) deep and shaped like the hull of a ship, was designed to float and move easily through the water.

Sponsons
These floats projected from the sides of the plane and balanced the aircraft on the water. They helped to give extra lift in the air, and were also used to hold fuel. Most other flying boats and seaplanes had floats under the wings.

PLANES THAT FLOAT

The huge flying boats of the late 1930s sped across the water on their take-off run. They established the first long-distance airline routes across the world's oceans. These journeys were beyond the range of conventional airplanes, which could not carry enough fuel. But flying boats were able to cross oceans by refuelling at harbours and islands as they went. The largest commercial flying boat was the Boeing 314, which entered service in March 1939.

During World War II (1939–1945), flying boats were used to hunt enemy submarines and rescue pilots. After the war, the flying boats found themselves competing with fast, reliable airliners on long-distance passenger routes. As the flying boats were much more expensive to run, they were gradually phased out.

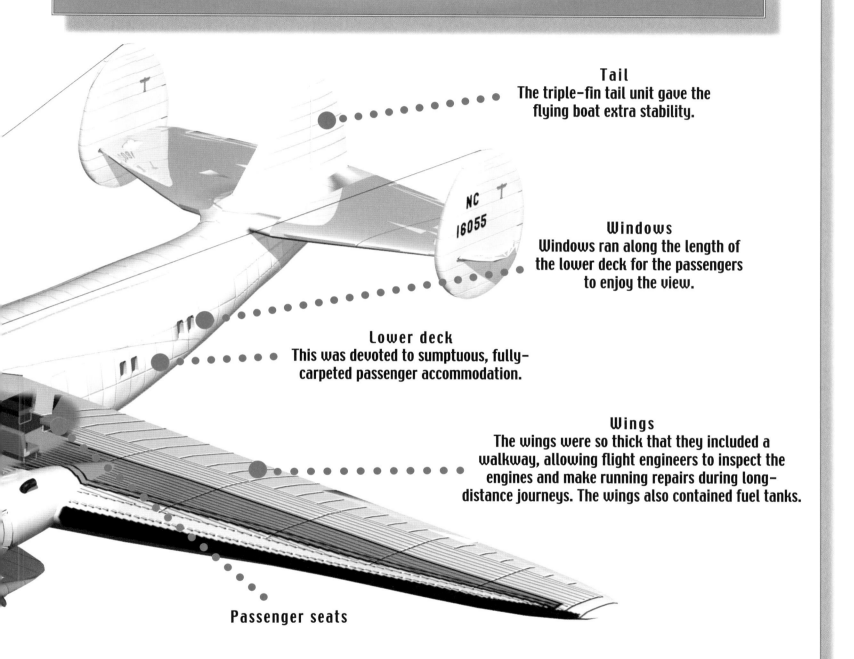

Tail
The triple–fin tail unit gave the flying boat extra stability.

Windows
Windows ran along the length of the lower deck for the passengers to enjoy the view.

Lower deck
This was devoted to sumptuous, fully–carpeted passenger accommodation.

Wings
The wings were so thick that they included a walkway, allowing flight engineers to inspect the engines and make running repairs during long–distance journeys. The wings also contained fuel tanks.

Passenger seats

THE MIGHTY CLIPPER

America's Boeing 314 was designed to carry around 75 day passengers, or 35–40 in sleeping berths on long-distance flights. The 10-man crew included two pilots, a navigator, a flight engineer, a radio operator, the ship's master (an officer who commanded the plane but did not fly it) and a relief crew of four.

Pan American Airways operated a fleet of Boeing 314s – called 'Clippers' after the fast sailing vessels of the nineteenth century – on routes across the Atlantic and Pacific. A Clipper's transatlantic journey from New York to Europe took about 24 hours, including two stops en-route. The flight across the Pacific, from San Francisco to Hong Kong, took five or six days, with rest and refuelling stops on Hawaii and other Pacific islands.

BOEING B-17 FLYING FORTRESS

Engine power
The B-17 had four turbocharged, air-cooled Wright R-1820-97 Cyclone engines. They were radial engines, which means that their nine cylinders were arranged in a circle around the crankshaft. Each gave 1,200 horsepower, allowing the B-17 to reach a maximum speed of just over 460 kph (285 mph). The cruising speed with a full bomb load was around 240 kph (150 mph).

Bombardier
Sitting in the nose of the plane, the bombardier used a bomb-sight to look through the flat viewing panel in the plastic cone and make sure that the bombs were released at just the right moment. Under fire from anti-aircraft guns or enemy fighters, the bombardier needed a steady nerve to hit the target.

Nose cone
This was made of single-piece moulded plastic and fitted with machine guns, one on either side.

Chin turret
The twin guns were remote-controlled from inside the nose cone.

Astro-navigation dome
For night-flying missions, the navigator would look out of this dome to check star positions.

Dorsal gun-turret
Mounted on top of the flight deck, this turret gave protection against fighters diving out of the Sun.

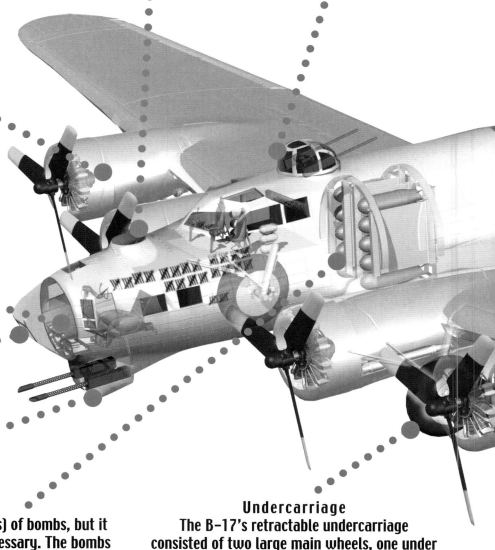

Bombs
The B-17 normally carried 2.7 tonnes (2.7 tons) of bombs, but it could manage up to 6.2 tonnes (6.1 tons) if necessary. The bombs were held in vertical racks in the bomb bay.

Undercarriage
The B-17's retractable undercarriage consisted of two large main wheels, one under each wing, and a smaller one near the tail.

BRISTLING WITH GUNS
World War II saw fighters and bombers develop by leaps and bounds to become fearsome military weapons. Huge formations of bombers caused massive destruction, and one of the most successful was the American Boeing B-17. Bombers were much slower than fighters and so were sitting targets for fast, agile enemy planes armed with machine guns and cannons. To counteract this threat, machine guns were mounted in almost every conceivable position on the B-17. In fact, the B-17 so bristled with armaments that one newspaper reporter called it a 'flying fortress' – and the name stuck!

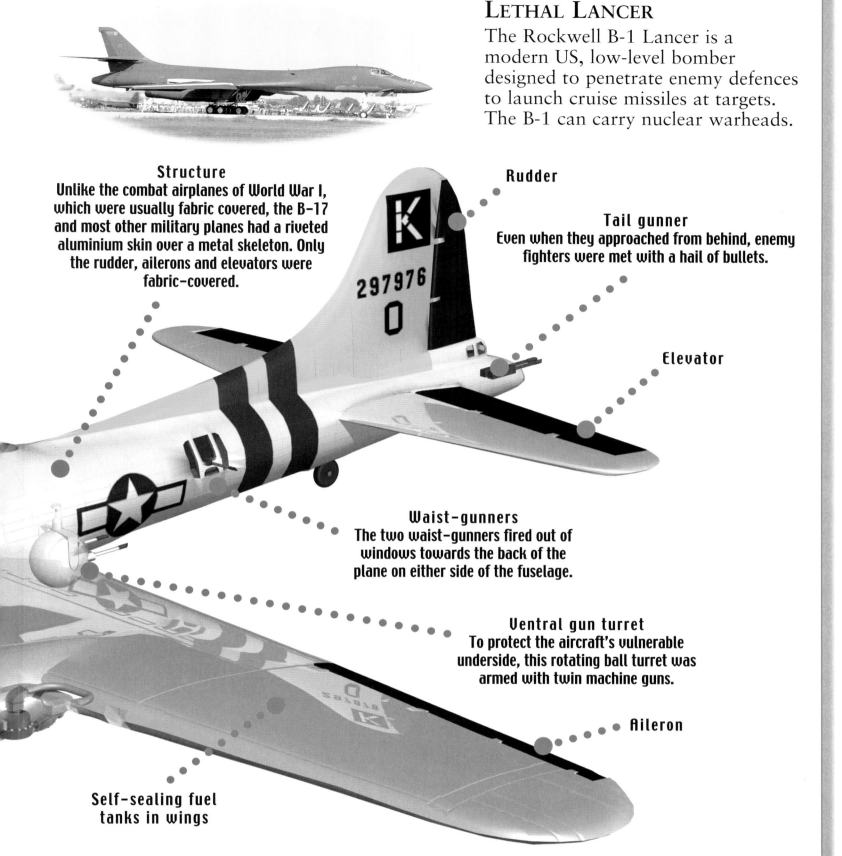

LETHAL LANCER
The Rockwell B-1 Lancer is a modern US, low-level bomber designed to penetrate enemy defences to launch cruise missiles at targets. The B-1 can carry nuclear warheads.

Structure
Unlike the combat airplanes of World War I, which were usually fabric covered, the B-17 and most other military planes had a riveted aluminium skin over a metal skeleton. Only the rudder, ailerons and elevators were fabric-covered.

Rudder

Tail gunner
Even when they approached from behind, enemy fighters were met with a hail of bullets.

Elevator

Waist-gunners
The two waist-gunners fired out of windows towards the back of the plane on either side of the fuselage.

Ventral gun turret
To protect the aircraft's vulnerable underside, this rotating ball turret was armed with twin machine guns.

Aileron

Self-sealing fuel tanks in wings

DAYLIGHT DANGER
Thousands of B-17s took part in daylight bombing raids over Europe, dropping more than 580,600 tonnes (571,450 tons) of high explosives on enemy targets. But daylight bombing made them vulnerable and initially many fell victim to German fighters. The B-17s' best defence was for large numbers of planes to fly in tight formation, so that fighters attacking from any direction faced a volley of fire from several aircraft. Flying like this, they managed to shoot down countless enemy planes.

The introduction of long-range escort fighters, such as the American P-51 Mustang, turned the tables. This allowed the B-17s to concentrate on their bombing missions while the escorts – their 'little friends', as the B-17 crews called them – dealt with enemy fighters.

BOEING 747- 400 'JUMBO JET'

Class act
As in most airliners, there are different classes of seats, all priced differently and offering different levels of comfort and service. The cheapest seats are economy class, with business class being more spacious, and first class offering the best facilities – and costing the most!

Fuel tanks
Situated in the wings and the tail-planes, the tanks hold over 216,840 litres (15,400 gallons) of fuel.

Flight deck
Dials and gauges have been replaced by six computer screens displaying all the key data the flight crew need to fly the plane. For most of the journey the computer 'autopilot' flies the plane, with the flight crew assuming control for take-off and landing. A relief crew of two may accompany the pilot and co-pilot on long-haul trips.

Washrooms
Passengers can freshen up on long, exhausting journeys.

Engine pods
The four pods suspended from wing pylons each carry a Rolls-Royce RB-211-524H turbofan engine.

Nose cone
This houses the weather radar scanner.

Galley
Meals are prepared on the ground before take-off and heated up in the galley during the flight.

THE JET AGE
In 1952, Britain's De Havilland Comet, the world's first jet airliner, entered service. The jet engine has no pistons but burns a fuel-air mixture in a combustion chamber. A jet of hot exhaust gases rushes out from the rear of the engine, providing thrust to push the plane forward. The air is squeezed by a compressor as it enters the engine. The compressor is driven by a set of turbine blades, which is why it is normally called a turbojet engine. Most modern jet engines have a huge fan in front to suck more air into the engine and give extra power. These are known as turbofan engines. They are quieter and burn less fuel than turbojets.

ELEPHANTINE AIRPLANE

As more people could afford to travel by air, ever more aircraft were needed to cope with the rising levels of passengers. To prevent the airports and skies from being gridlocked with air traffic, wide-bodied, high-capacity jets were developed. Foremost among the wide-bodied jets is the Boeing 747, nicknamed the 'Jumbo' because of its huge size. When it entered service in 1970, it was twice as heavy and powerful as any other airliner, and could carry double the number of passengers. The 747-400, the most recent model, carries just over 420 passengers on long-haul international flights, not forgetting all their luggage, plus fuel for the plane and food for the journey, and the crew.

Passenger cabin
The cabin is pressurized so that the passengers can breathe air normally. Emergency oxygen masks automatically drop from above if the cabin pressure is lost. Passengers sit in rows of seats, which can recline to let people sleep. Small items of baggage can be stored in overhead lockers.

Fuselage
On the inside of the fuselage is a thick insulating blanket that keeps out the cold and cuts out most of the noise from the engines.

Airline livery
The tail fin usually carries the logo or colours of the airline that owns the plane. This is known as the livery.

Wings
The 747's hollow wings, with a skin of aluminium alloy, contain the fuel tanks. The wings must be not only extremely strong to take the strain of the plane's vast weight, but also flexible enough to bend in strong winds without breaking. They are swept back to give the plane a more streamlined shape.

Winglets
These small turn-ups at the ends of the wings, 1.8 metres (5 feet) high, reduce drag around the wing tips, saving fuel and increasing the 747's range.

Hold
Underneath the passenger cabin is the cargo hold, where the passengers' luggage is stored in large containers during the flight.

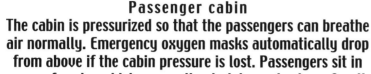

CONSTELLATION STAR

The 1940s saw a new generation of large passenger planes or 'airliners', which were propeller driven. The Lockheed Constellation was the first airliner with a pressurized cabin, enabling it to fly above bad weather and give passengers a more comfortable ride.

CONCORDE

Nose section
When taking off or landing, Concorde flies at a comparatively steep angle, with its nose in the air. To improve visibility from the cockpit, the hinged nose is lowered by 5 degrees for taxiing and take off, and 12.5 degrees when landing. For cruising, the nose is raised until it is straight.

Passenger cabin
Concorde's slender body can accommodate up to 128 passengers seated close together – far fewer than most modern long-distance airliners.

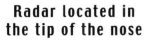

Radar located in the tip of the nose

Flight deck
The pilot and co-pilot sit side by side, facing the control panel, with the flight engineer behind them.

Galleys
Concorde has two galleys, one at the front of the plane and one at the rear. Six stewards serve the passengers meals of the highest quality.

Undercarriage
Concorde takes off and lands on 10 wheels fitted with multi-ply high-pressure tyres. There are four wheels on the landing gear under each wing, and two on the fuselage landing gear behind the nose.

THE NEED FOR SPEED

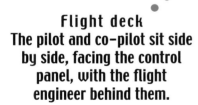

The fastest passenger plane in the world is Concorde, which can notch up an impressive 2,300 kph (1,430 mph). The fastest plane ever built, the North American X-15 rocket-powered research plane, flew more than three times faster than this!

SUPERSONIC MARVEL

Concorde is the world's fastest airliner. Jointly produced by Britain and France, Concorde is the only passenger plane that can fly faster than the speed of sound. Sound travels through the air at about 1,220 kph (755 mph) at sea level. But the speed of sound decreases with altitude as the air gets colder. A supersonic plane measures its speed with a Mach number, which is the plane's speed divided by the speed of sound at the height the plane is flying. Mach 1 is the speed of sound, Mach 2 is twice the speed of sound, and so on. Concorde's top speed is about Mach 2.2.

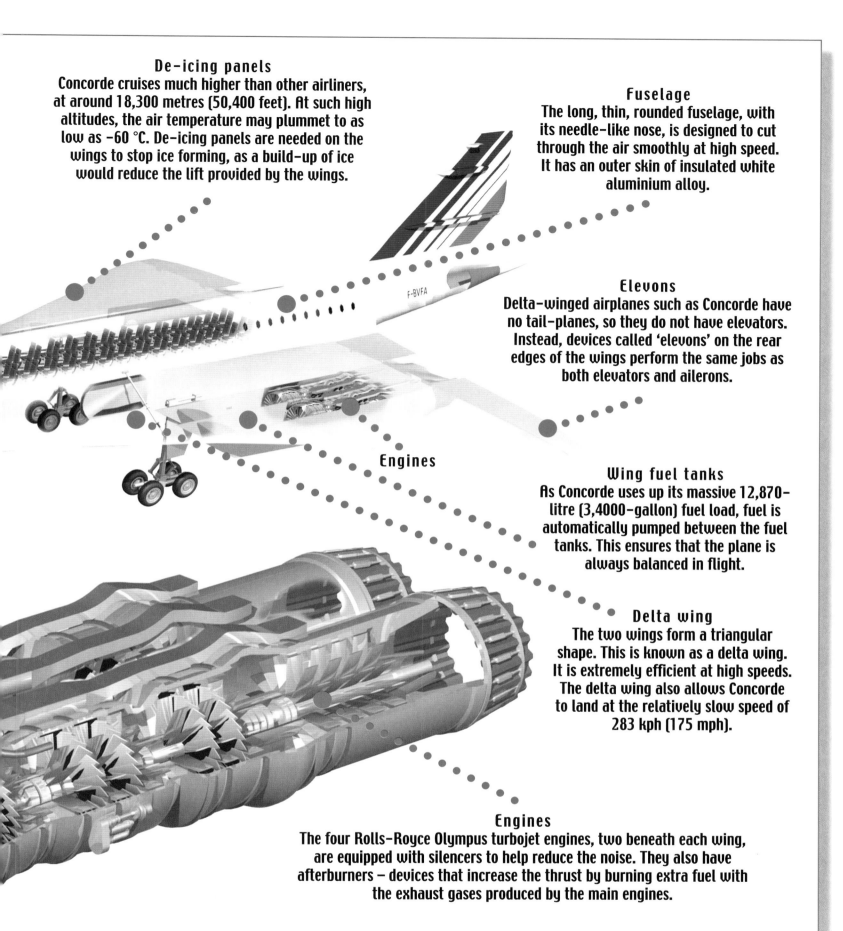

De-icing panels
Concorde cruises much higher than other airliners, at around 18,300 metres (50,400 feet). At such high altitudes, the air temperature may plummet to as low as –60 °C. De-icing panels are needed on the wings to stop ice forming, as a build-up of ice would reduce the lift provided by the wings.

Fuselage
The long, thin, rounded fuselage, with its needle-like nose, is designed to cut through the air smoothly at high speed. It has an outer skin of insulated white aluminium alloy.

Elevons
Delta-winged airplanes such as Concorde have no tail-planes, so they do not have elevators. Instead, devices called 'elevons' on the rear edges of the wings perform the same jobs as both elevators and ailerons.

Engines

Wing fuel tanks
As Concorde uses up its massive 12,870-litre (3,4000-gallon) fuel load, fuel is automatically pumped between the fuel tanks. This ensures that the plane is always balanced in flight.

Delta wing
The two wings form a triangular shape. This is known as a delta wing. It is extremely efficient at high speeds. The delta wing also allows Concorde to land at the relatively slow speed of 283 kph (175 mph).

Engines
The four Rolls-Royce Olympus turbojet engines, two beneath each wing, are equipped with silencers to help reduce the noise. They also have afterburners – devices that increase the thrust by burning extra fuel with the exhaust gases produced by the main engines.

UPS AND DOWNS OF SUPERSONIC FLIGHT

When an airplane travels faster than the speed of sound it creates a shock wave in the air that sounds like a tremendous echoing boom on the ground below. Because of this 'sonic boom', Concorde is not allowed to fly over some cities. The plane only attempts supersonic speeds over the ocean or when flying too high for the sound to be heard on the ground.

Everything in Concorde's design is geared towards making it as streamlined as possible to keep drag to a minimum at supersonic speeds. This is why the fuselage is so narrow, making seating in the passenger cabin cramped. But business people and VIPs are happy to pay Concorde's high prices for the convenience of travelling across the Atlantic in just 3.5 hours.

AIRBUS A300-600ST BELUGA

Cargo door
The Beluga's bulging 'forehead' is an upward–hinging door that is raised and lowered by hydraulic arms and secured by 24 latches. It is the largest door ever fitted to an aircraft.

Cargo bay
The vast cargo bay measures 37.7 metres (123 feet) long and 7.6 metres (25 feet) wide. As all the crew travel in the cockpit, the cargo bay does not need to be pressurized.

Loading cargo
Large items of cargo, such as fuselage parts, are manoeuvred to the open nose of the plane on a raised, mobile gantry and transferred into the cargo bay by conveyor belt.

Guide rails
The guide rails on the cargo bay floor assist loading.

Cockpit
The cockpit has a strengthened roof to support the front end of the cargo bay floor. There are two fixed seats for the pilot and co-pilot, and two folding seats for extra crew members.

Radome
The hinged nose tip houses weather radar.

Vital statistics
The Beluga is just over 56 metres (180 feet) long and more than 17 metres (47 feet) high. Unloaded, it weighs around 150 tonnes (148 tons).

CARGO CARRIERS

Planes designed to carry goods rather than passengers are called cargo or freight planes. The cargo can be anything from letters and parcels to emergency food supplies, military equipment such as tanks, and even parts of spacecraft. Some cargo planes are small light aircraft adapted to carry supplies to remote communities. Others are purpose-built workhorses of the air, such as America's Boeing C-130 Hercules, which has been ferrying cargo round the world since the 1950s. The record for the largest internal cargo bay belongs to the odd-looking Airbus A300-600ST Beluga, which has a capacity of around 1,400 cubic metres (1,100 cubic yards).

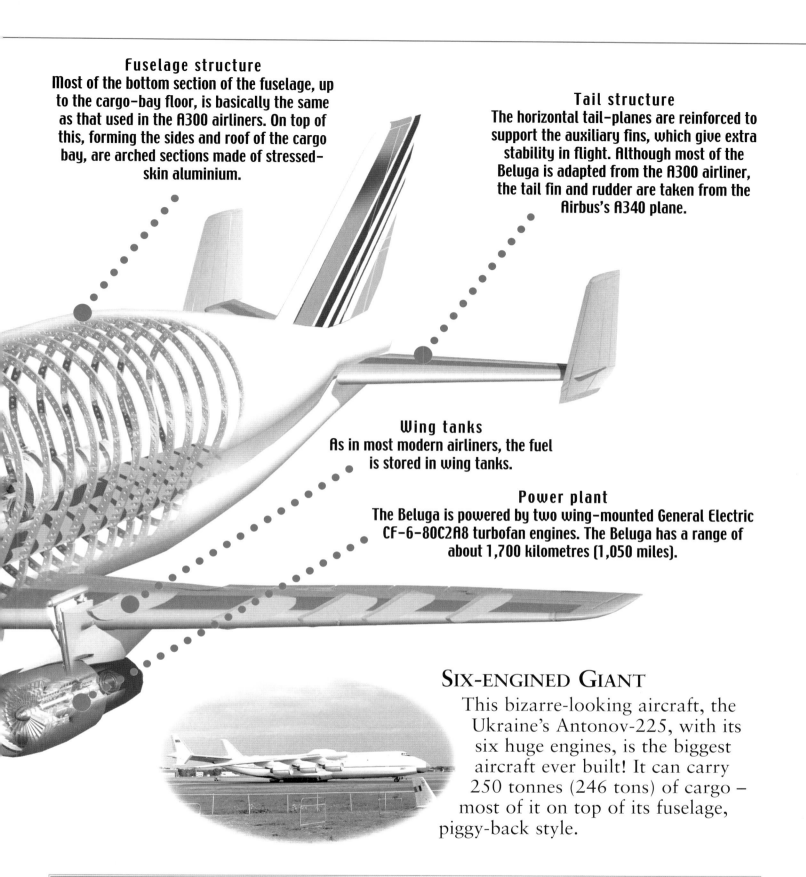

Fuselage structure
Most of the bottom section of the fuselage, up to the cargo-bay floor, is basically the same as that used in the A300 airliners. On top of this, forming the sides and roof of the cargo bay, are arched sections made of stressed-skin aluminium.

Tail structure
The horizontal tail-planes are reinforced to support the auxiliary fins, which give extra stability in flight. Although most of the Beluga is adapted from the A300 airliner, the tail fin and rudder are taken from the Airbus's A340 plane.

Wing tanks
As in most modern airliners, the fuel is stored in wing tanks.

Power plant
The Beluga is powered by two wing-mounted General Electric CF-6-80C2A8 turbofan engines. The Beluga has a range of about 1,700 kilometres (1,050 miles).

SIX-ENGINED GIANT

This bizarre-looking aircraft, the Ukraine's Antonov-225, with its six huge engines, is the biggest aircraft ever built! It can carry 250 tonnes (246 tons) of cargo – most of it on top of its fuselage, piggy-back style.

WHALE OF AN AIRCRAFT!

The Beluga, which entered service in 1996, is named after the white, bulbous-headed beluga whale. It was built by the European Airbus consortium as a 'super transporter' for carrying aircraft parts from their manufacturing sites around Europe to the assembly plant in Toulouse, France. The design for the Beluga was based on Airbus's successful A300 airliner. The cockpit was lowered and a new upper shell with a large front door was added. The tail fin was also changed to keep the plane stable when carrying heavy loads.

The Beluga is able to carry 45–50 tonnes (44–49 tons) in its cargo bay, which is big enough to transport large segments of fuselage for Airbus planes. Alternatively, it could hold a pair of wings for the A340 airliner or two pairs of A300 wings. The Beluga can also hold the complete first stage of the European Space Agency's Ariane 4 space rocket.

McDONNELL DOUGLAS AH-64 APACHE

Crew
The co-pilot/gunner sits in front of and below the pilot, in an armoured cockpit.

Power plant
Behind the rotor, and to either side of the fuselage, are the two 1,696 horsepower General Electric T700-GE-701C turbines. They give the Apache a top speed of around 300 kph (186 mph).

Main rotor
The four-blade rotor, with a diameter of 14.6 metres (40 feet), creates the helicopter's lift. The stainless steel and fibreglass blades have swept edges.

Controls
There are three main controls.
The control column is operated to tilt the main rotor to go forwards, backwards or sideways. The collective pitch lever is operated to change the pitch of the rotor blades, making the helicopter go up, down, or hover. Control pedals in the floor adjust the pitch of the tail-blades to turn left or right.

Nose assembly
The all-weather, day and night weapon-sighting equipment is mounted in the nose, and includes a TV camera, laser tracker, and forward-looking infrared sensor.

Chin gun
Aimed by the co-pilot/gunner, the 30-millimetre M230 Chin Gun has 1,200 rounds of ammunition.

Weaponry
The stubby wings provide four 'hard points' to which weapons can be attached. The Apache's favoured armoury is Rockwell AGM-114 Hellfire anti-tank missiles and rocket launchers loaded with 70-millimetre FFAR rockets. Usually it carries a combination of both. Extra fuel tanks or alternative armaments could also be attached to the hard points.

AWESOME APACHE

The Apache is a two-seat, anti-tank attack helicopter whose armoury can include guns, missiles and rockets. The helicopter can be a devastating weapon on the battlefield, hovering out of sight behind trees or buildings and then popping up unexpectedly to send a hail of rockets on to an enemy tank. Sometimes helicopters work in pairs, with one helicopter highlighting the target with a laser beam and guiding the other's missiles on to their target. Equipped with sensitive electronic devices, it can fight in daytime, at night, and in poor weather.

ROTARY WINGS

Helicopters are the most versatile of all aircraft, able to hover, take off and land vertically, and fly backwards and sideways, as well as forwards. Their rotor blades are like spinning wings. The blades are aerofoil-shaped and slightly angled. The angle of the blades is known as the pitch. The whirring blades push the air downwards and generate lift. The steeper the pitch of the blades, the greater the lift they give. When the lift is greater than the helicopter's weight, the aircraft takes off. When lift and weight are equal, the helicopter hovers, and when weight is greater than lift, the helicopter descends.

Using the controls, the pilot tilts the entire set of rotor blades forwards, giving thrust that pushes the helicopter along. To move sideways or backwards, the pilot simply tilts the blades in the desired direction. Changing the pitch of the tail-rotor blades turns the helicopter left or right.

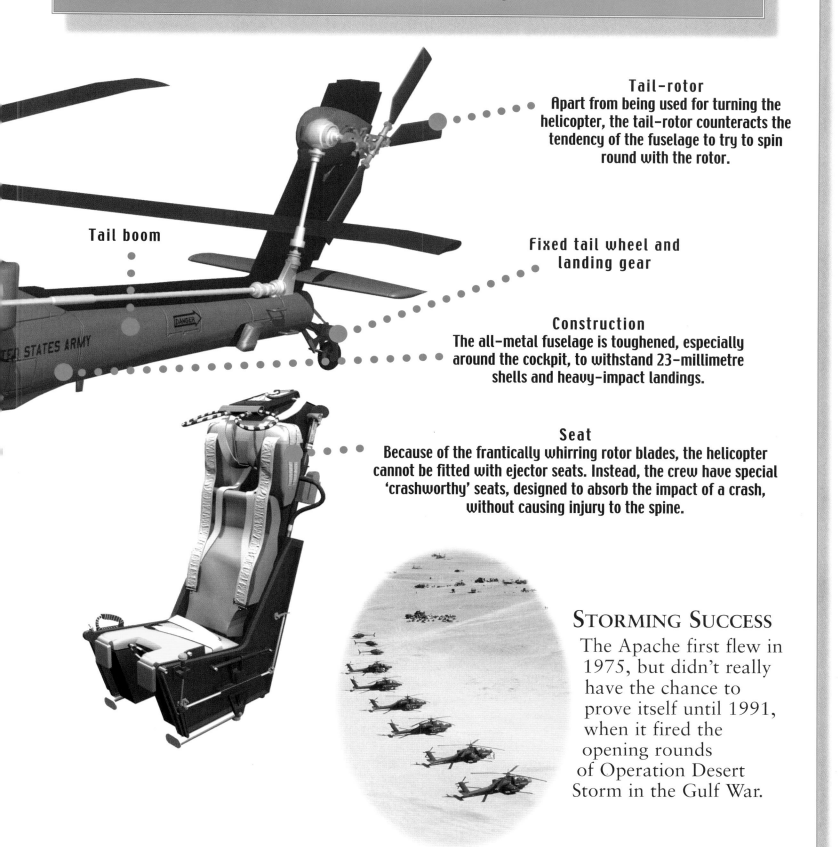

Tail-rotor
Apart from being used for turning the helicopter, the tail-rotor counteracts the tendency of the fuselage to try to spin round with the rotor.

Tail boom

Fixed tail wheel and landing gear

Construction
The all-metal fuselage is toughened, especially around the cockpit, to withstand 23-millimetre shells and heavy-impact landings.

Seat
Because of the frantically whirring rotor blades, the helicopter cannot be fitted with ejector seats. Instead, the crew have special 'crashworthy' seats, designed to absorb the impact of a crash, without causing injury to the spine.

STORMING SUCCESS

The Apache first flew in 1975, but didn't really have the chance to prove itself until 1991, when it fired the opening rounds of Operation Desert Storm in the Gulf War.

BOEING VERTOL CHINOOK CH-47

Capacity
The Chinook is extremely spacious inside, with a cabin measuring 2.3 metres (6 feet) wide, 2 metres (5 feet) high and over 9 metres (25 feet) long. It can carry 44 fully equipped troops or 24 injured soldiers on stretchers, along with medical attendants.

Turning technique
The fibreglass blades can spin at up to 225 times per minute. Because the Chinook doesn't have a tail-rotor, it needs another mechanism to turn the craft. Normally the speeds of the two rotors are the same so they balance each other out. But making one rotor spin faster or slower than the other turns the helicopter to the left or the right.

Cockpit
Two pilots and two crew sit in the cockpit. The cockpit seats have vibration absorbers to smooth the ride and reduce pilot fatigue. The flying controls are hydraulically powered.

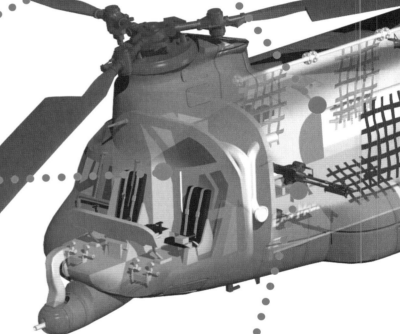

Weapons
The Chinook rarely carries weapons, but it can if necessary. Armaments can include machine guns, and grenade and rocket launchers.

Strong blast
The downrush of air from the Chinook's powerful rotors is equivalent to wind speeds of 90 kph (56 mph) – enough to blow a Cessna 172 on to its back!

WORKHORSE OF THE SKY

When you need to get large numbers of troops, emergency supplies or heavy machinery into awkward places – call for the Chinook! The 15-tonne (about 15-ton) Boeing Vertol CH-47 Chinook is probably the most reliable and popular heavy-lifting helicopter in the world. First introduced in 1961, it has been constantly updated and is still in service with most modern armed forces.

Under its belly, the Chinook has three crane hooks for lifting heavy objects. The front and back hooks can lift up to 5 tonnes (5 tons), but the central crane hook can raise loads in excess of 9 tonnes (9 tons), though not over great distances. The cargo is usually armoured vehicles, field guns and battlefield supplies. Three loads can be moved at once by using cables of different lengths so that the loads do not collide in flight.

Drive shaft
This carries power from engines to front rotor.

Deadly blades
The Chinook's rotor span is 18.3 metres (50 feet). Approach from the front and you risk decapitation, as the blades. can skim to 1.2 metres (3 feet) off the ground! At the rear, clearance is 5.4 metres (15 feet).

Engines
The twin Lycoming T55-L712 turbines give a top speed of 306 kph (190 mph). A compressor first squeezes the intake air. The air is then mixed with fuel, and the mixture burned in a combustion chamber. The waste gases drive a set of turbine blades which, in turn, power the rotors.

Cargo ramp
The ramp descends at the rear of the helicopter for fast loading and unloading.

Undercarriage
Two pairs of landing wheels give stability when the Chinook is fully laden.

Floating Wokka
The fuselage is watertight in case the Chinook comes down in the ocean.

Fuel supply
The large tanks under the cabin floor hold enough fuel for up to 10 hours flying, depending on the load.

BLACK HAWK
The Sikorsky Black Hawk is a multi-role transport helicopter, used to carry troops and equipment to the battlefield.

MIGHTY WOKKA!

The Chinook does not have a tail-rotor, but it counteracts the fuselage's tendency to spin round by having two very large main rotors, each turning in a different direction. The sound they make – a deafening 'wokka wokka' – is the origin of the Chinook's nickname: the Mighty Wokka.

The rotors are over 15 metres (41 feet) in diameter and actually overlap in the middle. The rear one is higher than the front one, and the two are linked by a gearing arrangement that ensures that they do not strike each other – which would be disastrous. The rotors are powered by two powerful engines at the rear of the helicopter. The Chinook has also been used as a passenger helicopter to make short trips between cities, and to carry personnel to and from oil rigs far out at sea.

SIKORSKY SEA KING

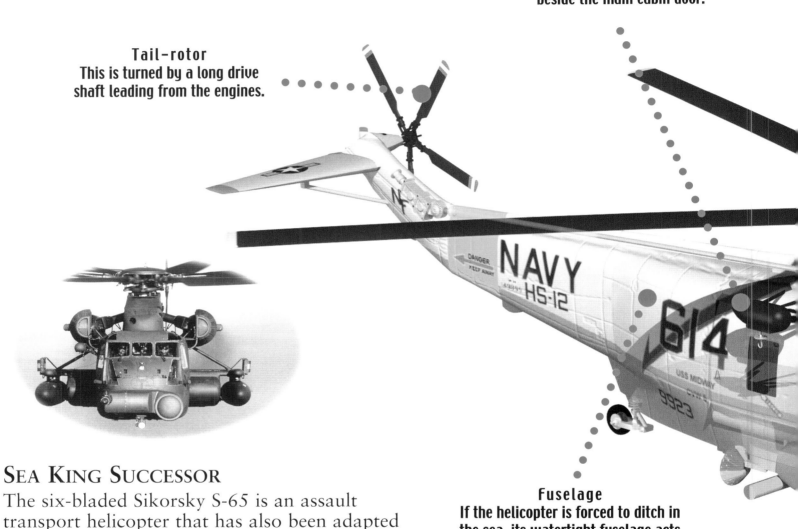

Winch
Search and rescue helicopters have a motor–driven winch, which raises and lowers a line running over a pulley beside the main cabin door.

Tail–rotor
This is turned by a long drive shaft leading from the engines.

Fuselage
If the helicopter is forced to ditch in the sea, its watertight fuselage acts like the hull of a boat and keeps it afloat for a while, giving the crew time to escape into life rafts.

SEA KING SUCCESSOR

The six-bladed Sikorsky S-65 is an assault transport helicopter that has also been adapted for mine sweeping and search and rescue (SAR) work at sea. In some countries it has replaced the Sea King as the main SAR helicopter.

FIRST AND FOREMOST

As long ago as 1483, the Italian artist and inventor Leonardo Da Vinci made drawings of a muscle-powered helicopter. It had a large, screw-like wing made of starched linen. Although the machine was never built and could not have flown in reality, his idea was way ahead of his time. It was more than 400 years later, in 1907, that Frenchman Paul Cornu made a 20-second hop in a twin-rotor helicopter, but the fragile craft broke apart when it landed with a bump. Helicopters only became truly practical with Russian-born Igor Sikorsky's VS-300 single-rotor craft, which was first flown in 1939. It may have looked cumbersome but it worked, opening a whole new chapter in the history of aviation. Sikorsky went on to produce a host of important helicopters, including the Sea King, famous for picking up US astronauts after splash-down in the ocean.

SEARCH AND RESCUE

The Sea King can perform daring rescue missions beyond the range of lifeboats, such as hoisting people off burning vessels at sea. With the helicopter hovering over the water, a crew member can be lowered on a winch to pluck drowning sailors from the waves. The Sea King is fully equipped with emergency medical supplies to help the injured, who can be lifted up into the helicopter in a sling or harness. The Sea King then whisks them back to shore at speeds of up to 230 kph (140 mph).

The Sea King made its maiden flight in 1959, and has been regularly updated ever since. It was originally designed as an anti-submarine helicopter, and is still used in that role today. Its other uses include airborne early warning (AEW) missions, transporting troops or civilian passengers, and taking personnel and supplies to off-shore oil rigs.

Main rotor
The main rotor has a span of 19 metres (52 feet). The five blades are hinged so that they can fold backwards if the helicopter needs to be stowed in a confined space.

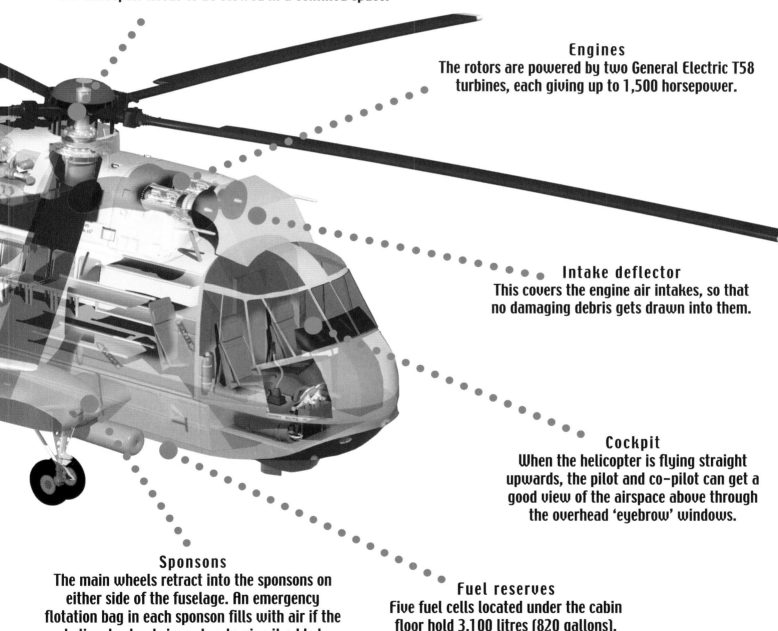

Engines
The rotors are powered by two General Electric T58 turbines, each giving up to 1,500 horsepower.

Intake deflector
This covers the engine air intakes, so that no damaging debris gets drawn into them.

Cockpit
When the helicopter is flying straight upwards, the pilot and co-pilot can get a good view of the airspace above through the overhead 'eyebrow' windows.

Sponsons
The main wheels retract into the sponsons on either side of the fuselage. An emergency flotation bag in each sponson fills with air if the helicopter lands in water, to give it added buoyancy.

Fuel reserves
Five fuel cells located under the cabin floor hold 3,100 litres (820 gallons).

BELL BOEING V-22 OSPREY

Wings
For storage aboard ships, the entire wing rotates through 90°. When the wing is lined up with the fuselage and the rotors are folded inwards, the Osprey's width is reduced from nearly 26 metres (85 feet) to just over 5 metres (16 feet).

Rotors
The three-bladed rotors are 11.6 metres (32 feet) in diameter and made of fibreglass and graphite. They are specially designed so that if they break off, they will not strike the cockpit or the passenger cabin.

Cockpit
The large, low-cut cockpit windows give excellent visibility. There are no ejector seats for the two pilots, but the cockpit is specially strengthened to withstand the impact of a crash.

Fly-by-wire
As with most modern combat aircraft, the Osprey uses computer-generated signals carried by electrical wires from the cockpit to activate the control surfaces, such as the elevators and flaperons.

Cabin
Along each wall of the cabin are a dozen impact-resistant seats, which are designed to absorb the shock of a bumpy touchdown or crash-landing.

Sponsons
Two bulging floats called sponsons, on either side of the fuselage, allow the Osprey to float on water. They carry more than 4,500 litres (320 gallons) of fuel, in addition to nearly 3,000 litres (210 gallons) held in self-sealing wing tanks.

TILT-ROTOR AIRCRAFT

For many years, designers dreamed of producing an aircraft that would combine the speed of an airplane with the manoeuvrability of a helicopter. The result is the Bell Boeing V-22 Osprey, a 'tilt-rotor' aircraft that can take off and hover like a helicopter and fly like a normal plane. The Osprey's secret lies in its engines, which can be swivelled to point either upwards or forwards.

The Osprey takes off with its engines and rotors pointing upwards to generate lift. With the Osprey airborne and hovering, the rotors and engines swivel into a horizontal, forward-facing position. The lift now comes from the wings, rather than the rotors, which provide the thrust to drive the plane forwards. The Osprey's rotors are so long that it cannot land like a normal airplane, as the rotors would strike the ground.

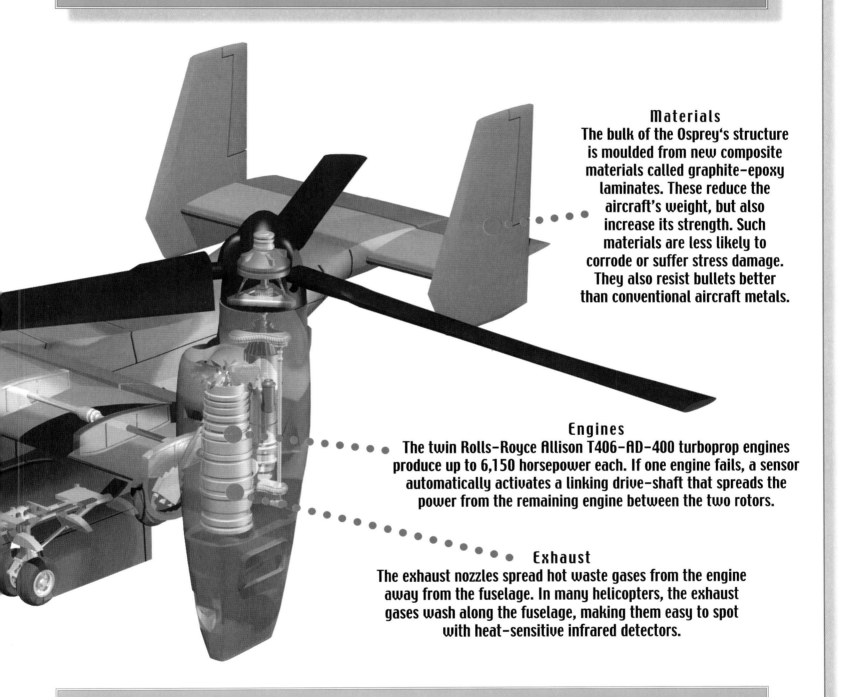

Materials
The bulk of the Osprey's structure is moulded from new composite materials called graphite-epoxy laminates. These reduce the aircraft's weight, but also increase its strength. Such materials are less likely to corrode or suffer stress damage. They also resist bullets better than conventional aircraft metals.

Engines
The twin Rolls-Royce Allison T406-AD-400 turboprop engines produce up to 6,150 horsepower each. If one engine fails, a sensor automatically activates a linking drive-shaft that spreads the power from the remaining engine between the two rotors.

Exhaust
The exhaust nozzles spread hot waste gases from the engine away from the fuselage. In many helicopters, the exhaust gases wash along the fuselage, making them easy to spot with heat-sensitive infrared detectors.

OSPREY IN ACTION

The Osprey was designed as a troop transporter, to launch quick assaults from ships against land-based targets. It can reach combat zones much faster than other helicopter transporters, carrying 24 fully equipped troops or 9,000 kilograms (4,090 pounds) of cargo. It can also be armed with a variety of weapons – from machine guns to anti-tank missiles, cannons and bombs – to operate as a 'gunship'. It can carry depth-charges and torpedoes to hunt and destroy enemy submarines. The Osprey could also be used by Coast Guard services for search and rescue missions at sea, as a reconnaissance aircraft, or even as an air ambulance.

CANADAIR CL-215

Windows
The large cockpit windows give all-round visibility, helping the pilot to aim the water drops accurately.

Power
The CL-215's powerhouses are two Pratt & Witney Canada 18-cylinder R2800 engines, which each produce 2,100 horsepower to drive the three-bladed propellers.

Chemical tanks
The CL-215 carries a special fire-fighting foam, which is stored in concentrated form in the plane's two chemical tanks.

Mooring pendant
To keep the plane steady when it rests on the water with its engines off, it can be moored to a jetty by a rope or cable attached to the pendant.

Nose undercarriage
Strong waterproof doors protect the steerable front wheels when they are withdrawn into the fuselage.

Drop doors
The water is dropped on to the fire by opening doors in the base of the water tanks.

Water tanks
The CL-215 can carry up to 5,346 litres (1,100 gallons) of water in its two storage tanks. The tanks can be filled by a hose before take-off.

WATER BOMBER

The Canadair CL-215 is designed specifically to reach forest fires quickly and get them under control. It quenches the flames by sweeping low over the blaze and 'bombing' them with huge quantities of water released from its water tanks. The plane refills by scooping up water from rivers and lakes. Flying at 130 kph (80 mph), with the fuselage skimming the water's surface, it can take just 10 seconds to fill the CL-215's tanks.

The CL-215 can fight fires for up to four hours before needing to refuel, making as many as 100 water drops and hurling nearly half a million litres (132,000 gallons) of water on to the blaze in a day.

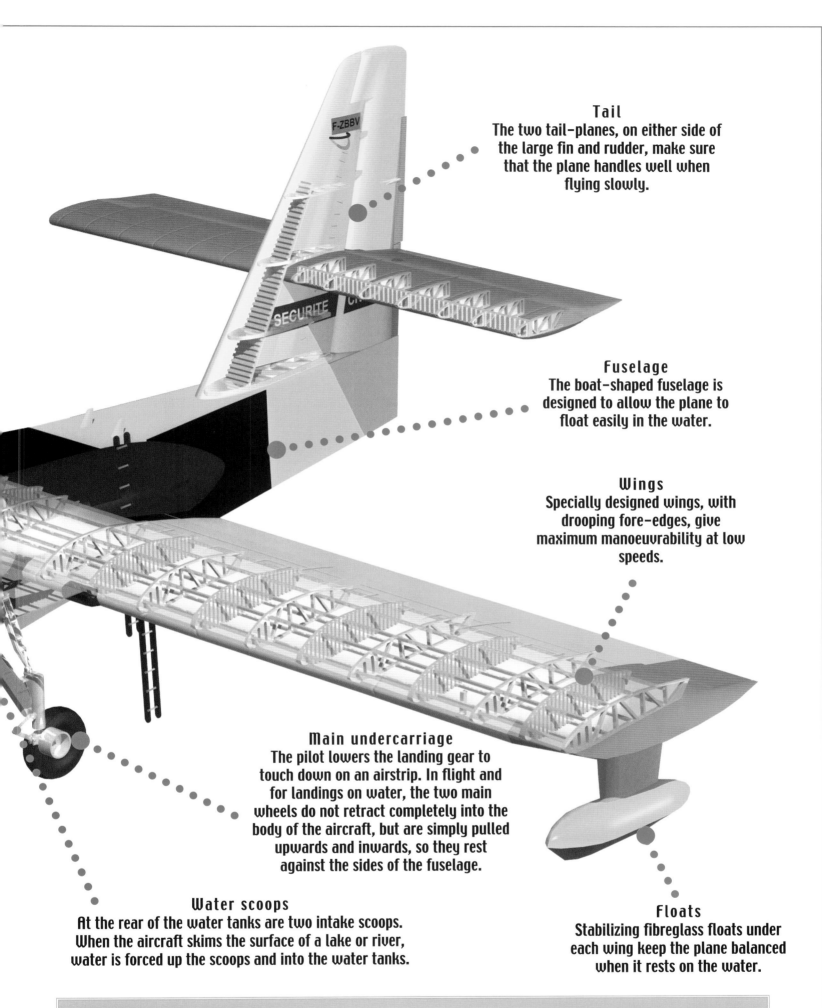

Tail
The two tail-planes, on either side of the large fin and rudder, make sure that the plane handles well when flying slowly.

Fuselage
The boat-shaped fuselage is designed to allow the plane to float easily in the water.

Wings
Specially designed wings, with drooping fore-edges, give maximum manoeuvrability at low speeds.

Main undercarriage
The pilot lowers the landing gear to touch down on an airstrip. In flight and for landings on water, the two main wheels do not retract completely into the body of the aircraft, but are simply pulled upwards and inwards, so they rest against the sides of the fuselage.

Water scoops
At the rear of the water tanks are two intake scoops. When the aircraft skims the surface of a lake or river, water is forced up the scoops and into the water tanks.

Floats
Stabilizing fibreglass floats under each wing keep the plane balanced when it rests on the water.

AERIAL FIRE-FIGHTING

Although the CL-215 can fight a fire with water alone, the best effects are produced using a fire-fighting foam. A small amount of a special chemical is added to the water as it is released from the tanks, forming a foam that expands as it falls. The foam blankets a large area of the fire, starving it of oxygen and extinguishing the flames. Foam is also dropped on to unburned trees around the blaze to prevent the fire from spreading.

BRITISH AEROSPACE /BOEING HARRIER

JUMP JET

In a tight dog-fight with enemy fighters, manoeuvrability is more valuable than speed. The Harrier is a V/STOL (Vertical/Short Take-Off and Landing) fighter and strike airplane. It can take off and fly straight upwards, and land by coming straight back down. If it has a heavy load, the Harrier takes a short run-up to help it 'jump' into the air.

Wings
The short, backward-sloping wings have a span of just 9.25 metres (25 feet). They are 'shoulder wings', which means that they are joined to the plane at the top of the fuselage.

Engine air-intake
There are two semicircular air-intakes, one on either side of the fuselage. A large fan at the front sucks air into the engine.

Engine
The Harrier is powered by a single Rolls-Royce Pegasus vectored-thrust turbofan engine located in the centre of the plane. Hatches just behind the cockpit give easy access for repairs and maintenance.

Nose cone
This contains sensors that can lock laser- and TV-guided weapons on to their targets.

Cockpit
The cockpit is equipped with a head-up display, video-screen information displays, a digital moving map, and night-vision goggles for the pilot.

Ejector seat
The pilot sits in a rocket-powered ejector seat unit, which has an oxygen mask, a parachute for descent to the ground and a rubber dinghy in case of a watery landing.

Cannon pods
The Harrier has two 30-millimetre cannon pods, one on each side of the plane's belly.

Main landing wheels
These descend from the centre of the fuselage.

Front engine nozzles
These expel cold air drawn in by the front fan.

Rear engine nozzle
These expel hot gases fr burning fuel in the engi

Materials
The Harrier's fuselage and wings are built from light, strong aluminium alloys and 'composite' materials such as carbon-fibre.

Avionics
Much of the 'hardware' for the electronic flight equipment, called avionics, is housed in the rear part of the fuselage.

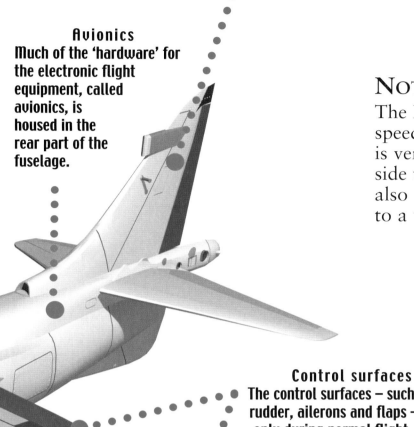

NOT FAST BUT DEADLY
The Harrier is not a fast airplane, with a top speed of about 1,200 kph (745 mph), but it is very agile. It can fly backwards, or from side to side, and it can even hover. It can also slow down from 1,000 kph (620 mph) to a virtual standstill in about 12 seconds.

Reaction jets
The main engine is too powerful for fine manoeuvres at low speeds, so the plane has small compressed-air 'puffers', called reaction jets. Located in the nose, wing-tips, and tail, the reaction jets are fed pressurized air from the compressor in the main engine.

Control surfaces
The control surfaces – such as the rudder, ailerons and flaps – work only during normal flight. At all other times, the plane is controlled by the engine nozzles and the reaction jets.

Wing wheels
Towards each wing-tip, away from the exhaust jets from the engine nozzles, the Harrier has a small wheel. Mounted on shock-absorbing legs, these wheels steady the plane during take-off and landing. The wheels fold back when the plane is flying.

Hard point/pylon
Missiles, bombs and extra fuel tanks are carried on the hard points (also called pylons). The Harrier can be fitted with up to nine hard points on the wings and fuselage.

VECTORED THRUST
The secret of the Harrier's success is its 'vectored thrust'. This is the ability to control and direct gases leaving the engine. The single jet engine has four rotating (vectoring) exhaust nozzles, just under where the wings meet the fuselage. For a vertical take-off, the nozzles point towards the ground, directing the gases downwards so that the plane is pushed up into the air. As the Harrier gains height, the nozzles swivel to point diagonally downwards, so that the gases push the plane both up and forwards. For normal flight the nozzles are directed backwards, and as the Harrier is propelled forwards the flow of air over the wings provides lift to keep the plane airborne. To fly backwards, the nozzles point down and slightly forwards.

A-10 THUNDERBOLT

Fuel tanks
The fuel is kept in special foam chambers that prevent fumes from forming. This lessens the risk of fire if the fuel tanks are damaged. The tanks are hidden right in the centre of the plane and protected by fire-detectors and extinguishers.

Canopy
The large bubble-shaped canopy gives good all-round vision. Its toughened glass can withstand small-arms fire.

Cockpit
The single pilot sits in a protective 'bathtub' made of ultra-strong titanium-alloy. The cockpit is filled with a host of switches, gauges and dials. During training, every pilot must pass a blindfold test in which they have to find and activate controls by touch alone.

Head-up display (HUD)
Modern combat aircraft often have a see-through screen that displays important flight information in front of the pilot's face. The pilot can read the details without having to look down at the flight instruments. HUDs can also be used for aiming guns or missiles at targets. Some pilot helmets have a special visor that does the same job as the HUD.

Boarding ladder

Ammunition belt and drum
Shells are fed to the cannon by the ammunition belt. The drum in the plane's belly carries 1,174 rounds of ammunition. It also collects the used shell-cases to prevent them flying into the engine's fans.

Rotary cannon
Slung beneath the cockpit is the single Avenger cannon, whose seven rotating barrels shoot bursts of high-velocity 30-millimetre high-explosive or armour-piercing shells. A short burst is all that is needed to put a tank out of action. The noise of the firing cannon gave it its nickname – the 'burp gun'.

ROVING DESTROYER
The A-10's role is to support ground forces. The A-10 entered service in 1976 and proved its worth to devastating effect in the Gulf War of 1990 and during the Kosovo conflict of 1999. The A-10 is slow compared to most combat airplanes, with poor acceleration, but the straight wings give tremendous lift and make it very agile at low speeds and low altitudes. They also allow it to take off and land on short runways built close to the combat zone. It can still fly with an entire engine shot off its mounting, one rudder missing, or a large chunk of a wing blown away in combat!

LINGERING THREAT

The A-10 lingers over the battlefield making low-level jinking runs, often at tree-top height, to attack tanks and other armoured vehicles.

Tail
The twin tail fins are designed to improve low-speed manoeuvrability. They also help to conceal the engine's hot exhaust gases from heat-seeking infrared missiles, making the A-10 a harder target for the missiles to lock on to.

Engines
The A-10 has two General Electric TF34-GE-100 turbofan engines mounted high on the rear of the fuselage so that the pilot has an unhindered view of the terrain below. The engines give the A-10 a top speed when fully loaded of 725 kph (450 mph) and a cruising speed of 555 kph (345 mph).

Ailerons
The special split ailerons help to stabilize the plane in flight as it blasts enemy tanks with its powerful cannon.

Weapons payload
The 11 pylons, three under the fuselage and four under each wing, can carry over 7,250 kilograms (3,300 pounds) of weapons or equipment. Weaponry can include rockets, air-to-air and air-to-ground guided missiles, and free-fall and guided bombs. The A-10 can also carry electronic countermeasures (ECM) pods, which contain transmitters that jam enemy radar.

Undercarriage
In flight, the wheels only partly retract. In the event of a crash-landing, they may help to lessen the impact, limiting damage to plane and pilot.

FLYING PIG

The pilots who fly the strange-looking A-10 nickname it the 'Warthog', after the fierce, ugly African wild pig. Like its animal namesake, the Warthog is not to be messed with. The A-10 was designed around its gun – a fearsome 6-metre (18-foot) long cannon that can spit out shells at a rate of up to 4,200 per minute. The cannon shoots straight ahead. This means that pilots have to fly directly towards targets, often facing flak (anti-aircraft fire) full on, so the A-10 needs to be tough – and it is! Titanium armour plating, up to 38 millimetres (1.5 inches) thick, surrounds the cockpit, and also helps to protect the engines and some of the flight control systems. The A-10 can survive direct hits from armour-piercing shells and high-explosive projectiles.

DAEDALUS PEDAL-POWERED PLANE

Wing-span
The huge wing-span allowed *Daedalus* to take off at speeds as low as 6.4 kph (4 mph), but meant it was likely to be thrown about by the gentlest winds. Kanellopoulos and his team waited in Crete for a month until the weather was calm enough to risk the flight.

Wing materials
The wings were made of styrofoam and balsa wood, with a main spar of carbon-fibre. They were strengthened by bracing wires and coated with mylar.

Vital statistics
During the flight, the 8.6-metre (24-foot) long *Daedalus* travelled about 5 metres (14 feet) above the water at an average speed of 30 kph (19 mph).

PIONEER OF PEDAL POWER

In April 1998, Greek cycling champion Kanellos Kanellopoulos pedalled a lightweight airplane across the Aegean Sea between the Greek islands of Crete and Santorini. The 119-kilometre (75-mile) flight, which took nearly four hours of non-stop pedalling, set a world record for human-powered flight. The airplane was named *Daedalus*, after the mythical Greek engineer who made wings of wax and feathers for himself and his son to escape from King Minos of Crete. *Daedalus* was built by a team of engineers at Massachusetts Institute of Technology (MIT), USA.

PEDAL-POWER PROBLEMS

The main problem with airplanes such as *Daedalus* is the lack of power. Pedalling constantly, Kanellopoulos averaged an output of just 0.27 horsepower – even the Wright brothers' *Flyer* produced 12 horsepower. The amazing flight was only possible because the plane had a wing-span as wide as a Boeing 727 airliner and weighed just 32 kilograms (70 pounds). The 34-metre (94-foot) wings gave tremendous lift, while modern, ultra-light materials kept the weight down. However, the huge wing-span made *Daedalus* unstable even in gentle winds, and Kanellopoulos fell into the sea just 10 metres (28 feet) short of his destination, when a gust of wind snapped the tail boom.

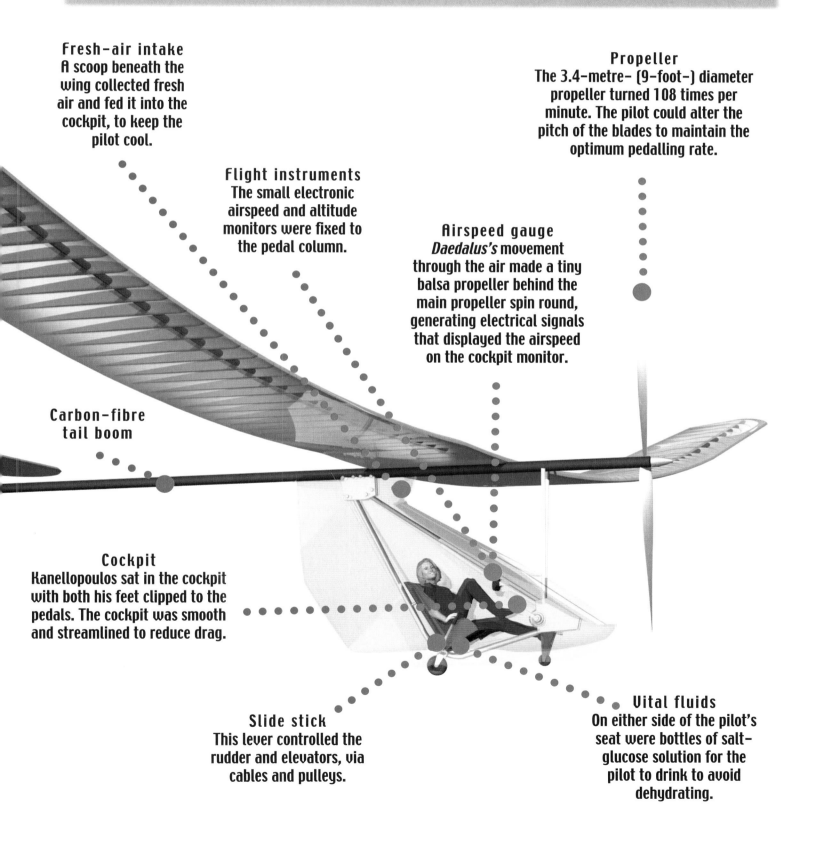

Fresh-air intake
A scoop beneath the wing collected fresh air and fed it into the cockpit, to keep the pilot cool.

Propeller
The 3.4-metre- (9-foot-) diameter propeller turned 108 times per minute. The pilot could alter the pitch of the blades to maintain the optimum pedalling rate.

Flight instruments
The small electronic airspeed and altitude monitors were fixed to the pedal column.

Airspeed gauge
Daedalus's movement through the air made a tiny balsa propeller behind the main propeller spin round, generating electrical signals that displayed the airspeed on the cockpit monitor.

Carbon-fibre tail boom

Cockpit
Kanellopoulos sat in the cockpit with both his feet clipped to the pedals. The cockpit was smooth and streamlined to reduce drag.

Slide stick
This lever controlled the rudder and elevators, via cables and pulleys.

Vital fluids
On either side of the pilot's seat were bottles of salt-glucose solution for the pilot to drink to avoid dehydrating.

GRUMMAN HAWKEYE

Rotodome
Measuring about 8 metres (22 feet) in diameter, the motor-driven radar disc, or 'rotodome', revolves five times per minute. Hydraulic jacks raise the rotodome for AEW patrols and lower it when the plane is out of action.

Fins and rudders
While the fuselage and wings are metal, the fins and rudders are largely fibreglass, to reduce radar reflection.

Chemical toilet
Even the best trained aircrew need to use the bathroom from time to time!

Control centre
The three systems operators – radar operator, air control officer and combat information officer – sit facing electronic display panels along the fuselage wall. The seats swivel to face forwards when taking off and landing.

Catapult tow-bar
Airplanes are launched from carriers by catapults, which hurl the planes from a standing start to speeds of around 320 kph (200 mph). For take-off, the tow-bar is attached to the catapult, which runs along a track in the deck.

SPY IN THE SKY
The Grumman Hawkeye is an airborne early warning (AEW) airplane. It may look as though it's carrying its own parasol, but the huge disc on top of the plane is actually a rotating radar antenna that scours the skies and seas for unfriendly intruders. Bristling with sophisticated electronic equipment, the Hawkeye can track over 2,000 aircraft, missiles, and ships simultaneously. It can detect and identify bomber-sized targets as far as 530 kilometres (330 miles) away – not bad for an airplane that made its maiden flight about 40 years ago! The E-2C II is the latest upgrade of the basic Hawkeye structure, and the Hawkeye 2000, currently under development, will continue to be the airborne eyes and ears of the US Navy for many years to come.

RADAR RECONNAISSANCE

The Hawkeyes travel with a fleet of naval ships on board an aircraft carrier. Once airborne, they can fly beyond the range of the carrier's own radar, giving a vast coverage of sky and sea. In a combat situation, they can give fighter pilots an idea of the 'big picture' of what's going on in an air battle, and alert them to threats and targets coming their way. The plane has a crew of five: two pilots, and three systems operators who analyse the data collected by the plane's monitoring equipment and communicate with the carrier and other aircraft.

Vital statistics
The Hawkeye is nearly 17.6 metres (48 feet) long, 5.6 metres (15 feet) high and has a wing-span of about 24.6 metres (8 feet).

Wings
When not in use, hydraulic jacks fold the wings back so that the Hawkeye does not take up too much space on the crowded carrier deck, and can fit on to the lifts that descend to the hangers below deck.

Engines
Two Allison T56-A-427 turboprop engines, mounted either side of the fuselage on the high, straight wings, drive the four-bladed composite propellers.

Cooling system
This intake duct houses the vapour-cycle radiator, which controls the temperature inside the plane. An efficient cooling system is needed, because the mass of electronic equipment on board the Hawkeye generates a lot of heat.

Hardware
The electronic hardware for all the Hawkeye's systems is packed into the area behind the pilot's cockpit.

Cockpit
The side windows bulge outwards so the pilots can get a good downward view. The windscreen is electrically heated, to prevent ice formation. Parachutes are located behind the pilots' seats.

GUIDE IN THE SKY

Hawkeyes are always the first planes to take off from an aircraft carrier and the last to land. They act as 'flying control towers' for other aircraft launched from the carrier, such as this Northrop Grumman F-14 Tomcat. The Hawkeyes guide their flight to and from the ship.

NORTH AMERICAN X-15

Wing jets
Like the nose jets, these helped to make minor adjustments to the X-15's flight. They controlled rolling.

Helium sphere
Helium gas from this sphere, at the rear of the aircraft, was used to keep the fuel tanks pressurized.

Heat dispersal
Friction with the air generated temperatures of almost 650 °C. The whole plane was coated with a special pink material (MA–25S) which 'boiled' away in flight, taking heat with it. Beneath this covering, the X–15 was spray-painted jet-black with a special silicone-based paint that helped to disperse heat.

Skin
The outer skin of the X-15 was made of special nickel-chromium alloy, called Inconel X, while most of the underlying structure was titanium alloy.

Rocket engine

X-PLANES

Many unusual-looking experimental aircraft, often called X-planes, have been built for research into high speed flight. One of the most famous X-planes was the Bell X-1. Flown by Captain Charles 'Chuck' Yeager, it became the first plane to fly faster than the speed of sound in October 1947, when it reached 1,078 kph (668 mph). Perhaps the most amazing X-plane of all was the dart-shaped North American X-15. This rocket-powered plane was used in the 1960s to investigate flight at hypersonic speeds (at least five times faster than the speed of sound).

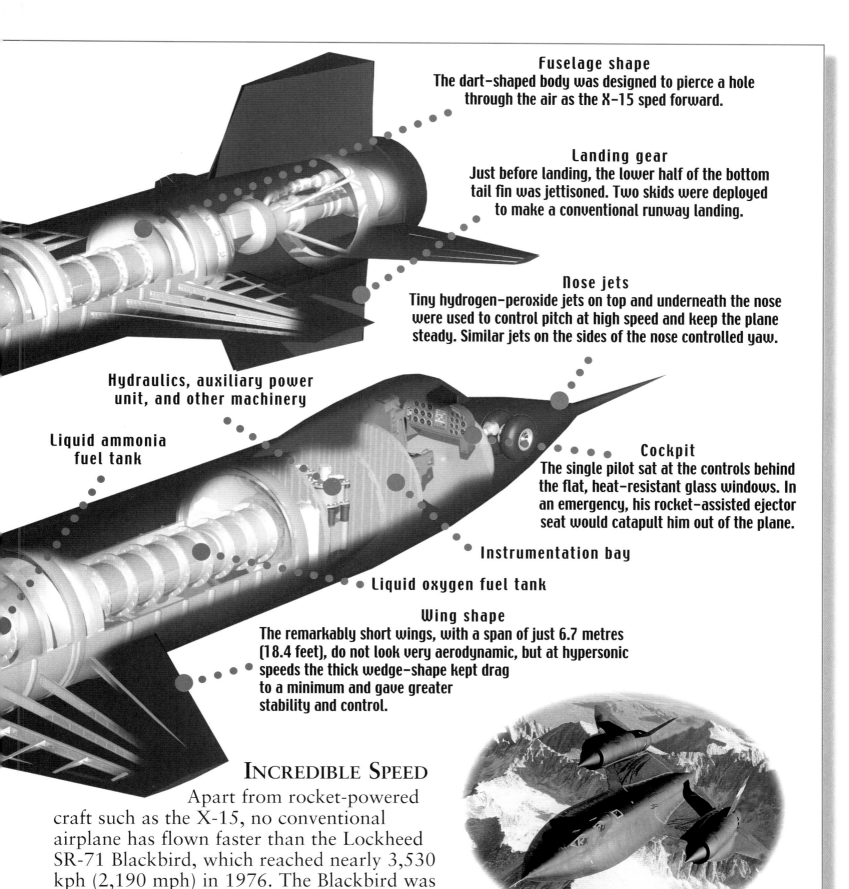

Fuselage shape
The dart-shaped body was designed to pierce a hole through the air as the X-15 sped forward.

Landing gear
Just before landing, the lower half of the bottom tail fin was jettisoned. Two skids were deployed to make a conventional runway landing.

Nose jets
Tiny hydrogen-peroxide jets on top and underneath the nose were used to control pitch at high speed and keep the plane steady. Similar jets on the sides of the nose controlled yaw.

Hydraulics, auxiliary power unit, and other machinery

Liquid ammonia fuel tank

Cockpit
The single pilot sat at the controls behind the flat, heat-resistant glass windows. In an emergency, his rocket-assisted ejector seat would catapult him out of the plane.

Instrumentation bay

Liquid oxygen fuel tank

Wing shape
The remarkably short wings, with a span of just 6.7 metres (18.4 feet), do not look very aerodynamic, but at hypersonic speeds the thick wedge-shape kept drag to a minimum and gave greater stability and control.

INCREDIBLE SPEED

Apart from rocket-powered craft such as the X-15, no conventional airplane has flown faster than the Lockheed SR-71 Blackbird, which reached nearly 3,530 kph (2,190 mph) in 1976. The Blackbird was used for secret reconnaissance missions by the US air force, but has now been withdrawn from service.

THE EDGE OF SPACE

The X-15 was carried into the air by a modified B-52 Stratofortress bomber and released at a high altitude. Once the X-15 was clear of the 'parent' plane, the pilot fired the rocket engine, which burned liquid ammonia fuel with liquid oxygen. With the rocket blazing, the X-15 climbed to the edge of the atmosphere, on the very fringes of space, where small jets in the nose and wings helped to keep it steady and on course. The X-15 made so many flights near to the edge of space that six of the 12 pilots qualified for astronaut's wings. Much of the technology that later went into making the Space Shuttle was tested on the X-15.

APOLLO 11 SATURN V ROCKET

Escape tower

Stage three
The third stage put the spacecraft into orbit and sent it heading towards the Moon. Its fuel tanks contained liquid hydrogen and liquid oxygen for its single engine.

Command and service modules
Having reached the Moon, the command and service modules remained in orbit, with Michael Collins aboard, while the LEM took Armstrong and Aldrin down to the lunar surface.

LEM

Docking manoeuvres
After separating from the third stage of the Saturn V rocket, the command and service modules had to turn round and dock with the LEM before continuing on to the Moon.

Main engine nozzle

Command module
The cramped command module was where the three astronauts lived and worked for most of the mission. It was the only part of the Saturn V rocket to return to Earth.

Service module
This contained life-support systems for the crew, such as oxygen for the astronauts to breathe and fuel cells that generated electricity to power Apollo 11's equipment. The fuel cells also converted hydrogen and oxygen into water for the astronauts to drink. The service module housed the engine for sending Apollo 11 back from the Moon.

THE SPACE RACE

In April 1961, Yuri Gagarin astonished the world by becoming the first person in space on board Vostok 1, the Soviet Union's rocket-launched spacecraft. Spurred on by the success of its arch-rivals, the US National Aeronautics and Space Administration (NASA) at once began work on the Saturn V moon rocket to put the first astronauts on the Moon.

This vast liquid-fuelled rocket was 111 metres (305 feet) high and weighed over 2,900 tonnes (2,850 tons). Early Apollo space missions tried out the Saturn V rocket, and on 16 July 1969, Saturn V launched Apollo 11 from Cape Canaveral, Florida, and headed for the Moon with astronauts Neil Armstrong, Buzz Aldrin, and Michael Collins on board...

MOON VOYAGE

The Saturn V rocket had three stages, each of which carried Apollo 11 further into space. As each stage used up its fuel, it was jettisoned. Only the command, service and lunar excursion modules continued on to the Moon. Once in orbit around the Moon, the lunar excursion module (LEM) separated and descended to the surface. Wearing protective suits, Armstrong and Aldrin explored the lunar landscape, gathering rock samples and setting up experiments.

After 22 hours, the top part of the LEM blasted off from the Moon's surface and rejoined the command and service modules in orbit. Armstrong and Aldrin were reunited with Collins, the LEM was jettisoned and Apollo 11 headed back to Earth. The command module separated from the service module before re-entering the atmosphere, and finally parachuting into the Pacific Ocean.

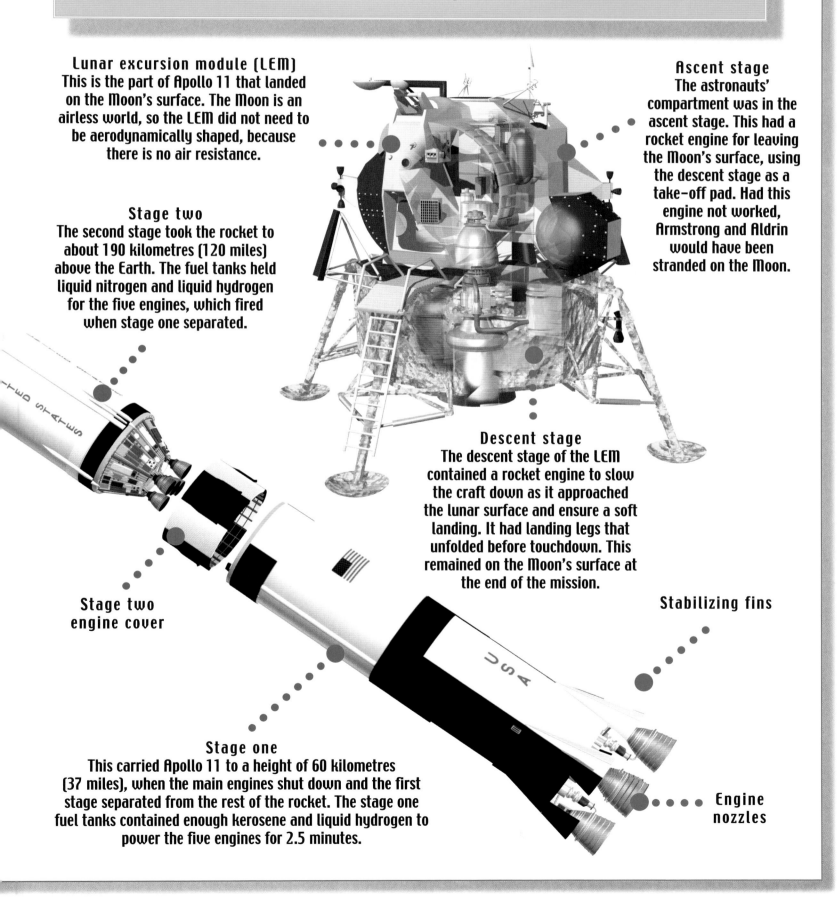

Lunar excursion module (LEM)
This is the part of Apollo 11 that landed on the Moon's surface. The Moon is an airless world, so the LEM did not need to be aerodynamically shaped, because there is no air resistance.

Stage two
The second stage took the rocket to about 190 kilometres (120 miles) above the Earth. The fuel tanks held liquid nitrogen and liquid hydrogen for the five engines, which fired when stage one separated.

Ascent stage
The astronauts' compartment was in the ascent stage. This had a rocket engine for leaving the Moon's surface, using the descent stage as a take-off pad. Had this engine not worked, Armstrong and Aldrin would have been stranded on the Moon.

Descent stage
The descent stage of the LEM contained a rocket engine to slow the craft down as it approached the lunar surface and ensure a soft landing. It had landing legs that unfolded before touchdown. This remained on the Moon's surface at the end of the mission.

Stage two engine cover

Stabilizing fins

Engine nozzles

Stage one
This carried Apollo 11 to a height of 60 kilometres (37 miles), when the main engines shut down and the first stage separated from the rest of the rocket. The stage one fuel tanks contained enough kerosene and liquid hydrogen to power the five engines for 2.5 minutes.

SPACE SHUTTLE

Tiled surface
On re-entry, friction between the orbiter and the Earth's atmosphere heats the outside of the craft to as much as 1,500 °C. Much of the orbiter's surface is covered by a protective layer of silica-fibre tiles, which fit together like the pieces of a jigsaw. The tiles absorb heat and prevent the orbiter from melting. The tip of the nose and the wings' leading edges get hottest, so they are also coated with a special type of carbon for extra heat insulation.

Flight deck
The pilot and mission commander sit on the flight deck. There are also two seats for specialist astronauts who may need to be on the flight deck during the mission.

Structure
The 37-metre- (100-foot-) long orbiter has a construction similar to a normal airplane, with a framework made of light aluminium alloy.

Space laboratory

Robot arm
Controlled from inside the orbiter, this long jointed arm can lift satellites out of the payload bay and recapture them in orbit.

Mid-deck
During the mission, which may last up to 16 days, the living area for the seven astronaut crew is the mid-deck. Some sleeping berths are horizontal and others are vertical, but it doesn't really matter in a weightless environment. There is also a washroom, a galley and an airlock allowing access into the unpressurized payload bay.

Windows
The heat-resistant, triple-glazed windows are 65 millimetres (2.5 inches) thick.

Thrusters
Small adjustments to the craft's orbit can be made by firing different combinations of the 44 jet thrusters.

Discovery

Lower deck
The crew's life-support systems are housed in the orbiter's lower deck. Air-filters remove carbon dioxide and water vapour breathed out by the astronauts, keeping the air breathable.

LAUNCHING THE SHUTTLE

The speed needed to get into orbit around the Earth is an astonishing 28,080 kph (17,410 mph). To achieve this, the Shuttle's three main engines need the help of two solid-fuel boosters. These five engines produce as much power as more than 140 Boeing 747 jumbo jets! At an altitude of 45–50 kilometres (around 30 miles), the boosters shut down and fall back to Earth, slowed by parachutes. They drop into the ocean, to be recovered and used again.

A fuel tank attached to the bottom of the orbiter carries liquid hydrogen and liquid oxygen for the main engines to burn. After eight minutes, and a height of about 110 kilometres (68 miles), the fuel tank is jettisoned and burns up in the atmosphere. Less than 10 minutes after blast-off, the craft is in orbit.

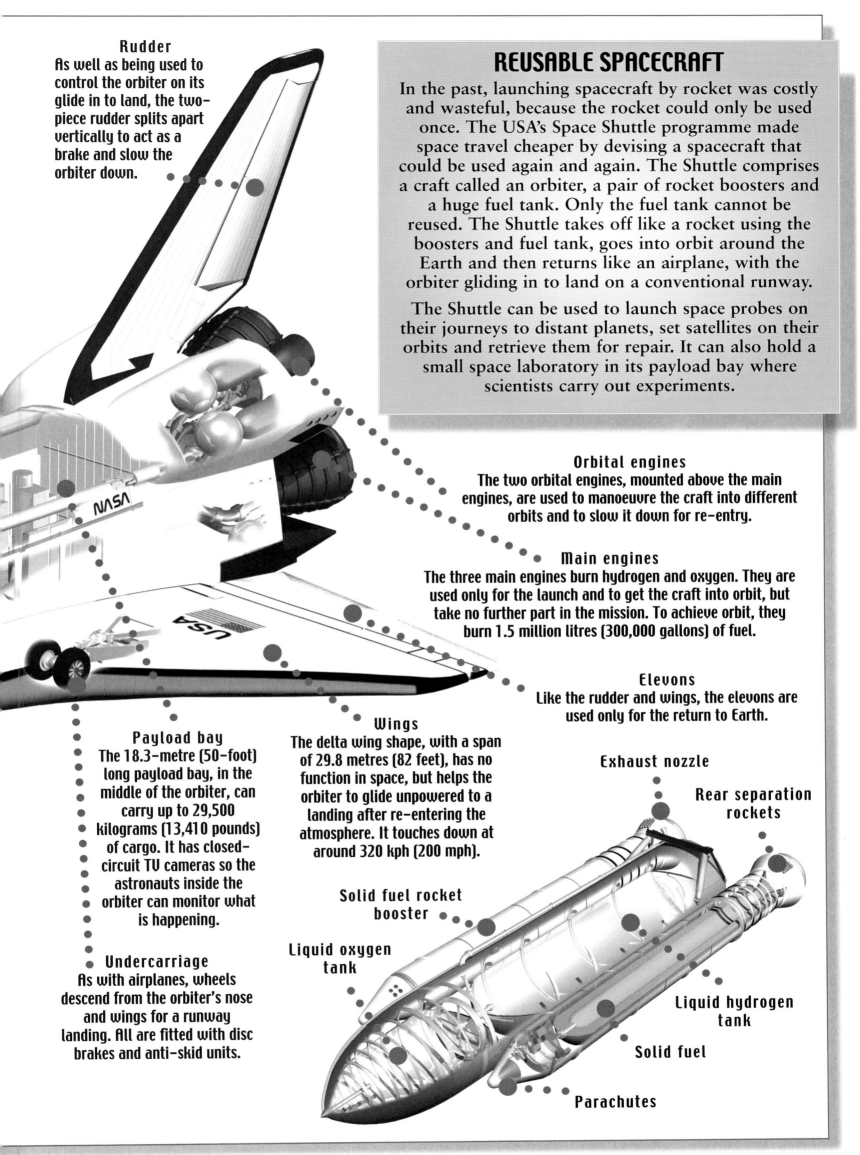

Rudder
As well as being used to control the orbiter on its glide in to land, the two-piece rudder splits apart vertically to act as a brake and slow the orbiter down.

NASA

NASA

USA

REUSABLE SPACECRAFT
In the past, launching spacecraft by rocket was costly and wasteful, because the rocket could only be used once. The USA's Space Shuttle programme made space travel cheaper by devising a spacecraft that could be used again and again. The Shuttle comprises a craft called an orbiter, a pair of rocket boosters and a huge fuel tank. Only the fuel tank cannot be reused. The Shuttle takes off like a rocket using the boosters and fuel tank, goes into orbit around the Earth and then returns like an airplane, with the orbiter gliding in to land on a conventional runway.

The Shuttle can be used to launch space probes on their journeys to distant planets, set satellites on their orbits and retrieve them for repair. It can also hold a small space laboratory in its payload bay where scientists carry out experiments.

Orbital engines
The two orbital engines, mounted above the main engines, are used to manoeuvre the craft into different orbits and to slow it down for re-entry.

Main engines
The three main engines burn hydrogen and oxygen. They are used only for the launch and to get the craft into orbit, but take no further part in the mission. To achieve orbit, they burn 1.5 million litres (300,000 gallons) of fuel.

Elevons
Like the rudder and wings, the elevons are used only for the return to Earth.

Payload bay
The 18.3-metre (50-foot) long payload bay, in the middle of the orbiter, can carry up to 29,500 kilograms (13,410 pounds) of cargo. It has closed-circuit TV cameras so the astronauts inside the orbiter can monitor what is happening.

Wings
The delta wing shape, with a span of 29.8 metres (82 feet), has no function in space, but helps the orbiter to glide unpowered to a landing after re-entering the atmosphere. It touches down at around 320 kph (200 mph).

Undercarriage
As with airplanes, wheels descend from the orbiter's nose and wings for a runway landing. All are fitted with disc brakes and anti-skid units.

Exhaust nozzle

Rear separation rockets

Solid fuel rocket booster

Liquid oxygen tank

Liquid hydrogen tank

Solid fuel

Parachutes

CASSINI/ HUYGENS SPACE PROBE

Radio antenna dish
When Cassini is orbiting Saturn, it will be between about 760–950 million kilometres (470–590 million miles) from Earth. Radio signals will take up to 84 minutes to travel between Earth and Cassini. So if anything unexpected happens to the probe, it will be three hours before mission controllers on Earth are aware of it.

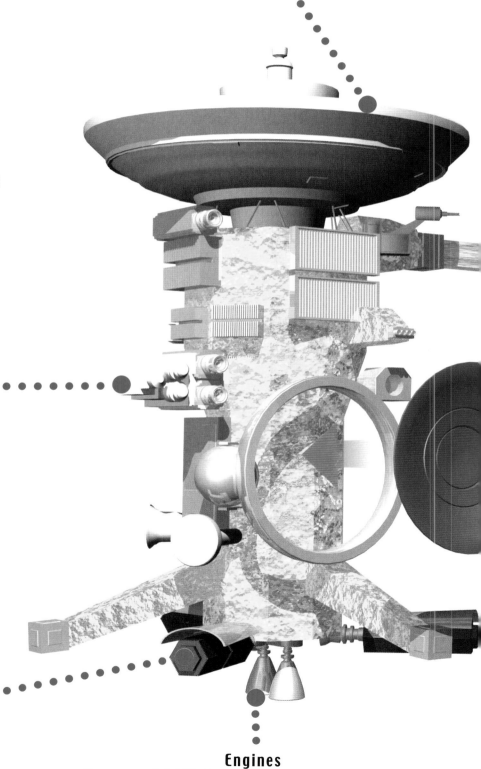

Equipment pallet
Huygens has two 'pallets', one on either side of the craft, laden with equipment for scientific experiments. It will map surface features by radar, analyse cosmic dust, take pictures in visible, ultraviolet and infrared light, and study the gravity of Saturn and its moons.

Nuclear power source
Cassini's equipment and systems are powered by its own nuclear generators. Some probes use solar panels, which harness the energy of the Sun, as their power source. This would not be practical for Cassini, as Saturn is too far from the Sun.

Engines
Two powerful 445-N engines give propulsion for major changes to Cassini's course. Sixteen small jet-thrusters make minor alterations to the probe's flight path.

SPECTACULAR SCIENCE

In November 2004, Huygens will detach from Cassini. Three weeks later it will land on Titan, the largest of Saturn's 18 moons. A heat shield will prevent the probe burning up as it enters Titan's atmosphere, then Huygens will parachute to the surface through the thick orange clouds.

On-board instruments will photograph and sample the surface and atmosphere, measure winds and relay data to the Cassini orbiter, which will transmit it back to Earth. Because Titan's atmosphere is mostly nitrogen gas, like the Earth's, scientists hope that Huygens' experiments will help them to understand more about how life began on Earth.

Magnetometer boom
This can detect and measure the strength of a planet's magnetic field.

Heat shield
The heat shield, 2.7 metres (7.4 feet) in diameter, will have to withstand temperatures of up to 2,000 °C as the probe enters Titan's atmosphere. The delicate scientific equipment underneath will be damaged if Huygens' internal temperature exceeds 180 °C.

PROBING THE SOLAR SYSTEM

Using on-board cameras and scientific instruments, space probes send back pictures and data that teach us about our Solar System. Launched by a rocket or the Space Shuttle, a space probe can use a technique called 'gravity assist' to help it reach its target. This involves flying close to another planet so that its gravitational field accelerates the probe and changes its direction. Like a slingshot, the planet's gravity hurls the probe out into space again on a new course.

NASA's Cassini orbiter probe was launched in 1997. It carries a smaller lander probe, called Huygens, built by the European Space Agency (ESA). After four gravity assist flybys – two at Venus, and one each at Earth and Jupiter – Cassini will reach Saturn in 2004 and will spend four years studying the planet.

Descent module
Beneath Huygens' heat shield is the descent module, which consists of two platforms within an aluminium shell. The upper platform holds communications antennae and parachutes. The lower platform holds all the scientific equipment for testing Titan's atmosphere.

Huygens probe
Huygens is secured to Cassini in a ring-like harness by exploding bolts. Approaching Titan, the bolts will be fired, freeing Huygens from the harness. Springs and rollers will then eject Huygens and send it spinning towards Titan.

FANTASTIC FUTURE

It is only about 100 years since the age of powered flight began with the Wright brothers' Flyer. Yet in that time, aircraft have revolutionized the way we live and taken us to new parts of the Solar System. It is difficult to predict what the flying machine of the future will be like, but one thing is for sure: there will be ever increasing numbers of people wanting to travel, and wanting to get to where they're going more quickly and more cheaply.

RETURN OF THE AIRSHIP

Airships were the wonders of the skies in the past, and they could be again in the future. A new generation of airships is now being designed, some of which will be huge cargo-lifters, rather like flying cranes, with the load suspended beneath the airship. Others will be moored over major cities and act as airborne telecommunications stations. There are even plans to produce passenger airships to take tourists on sky cruises.

Airliners
We may see a new range of 'jumbo' Jumbo jets, such as the planned Airbus A3XX, which could carry an incredible 658 passengers, or perhaps a new generation of supersonic airliners – although the development costs of Concorde and the noise problems it creates have put off many aircraft developers.

Robot planes
The fighters and strike planes of the future may be pilot-less robot vehicles. Directed by computer operators in a mission control station – either on the ground, in a ship or in another aircraft – these small, light planes could undertake daring raids with no risk to air crew. They could perform all the current roles of combat aircraft and carry out much more extreme aerial manoeuvres, without worrying about the stresses and strains they put on the pilot's body.

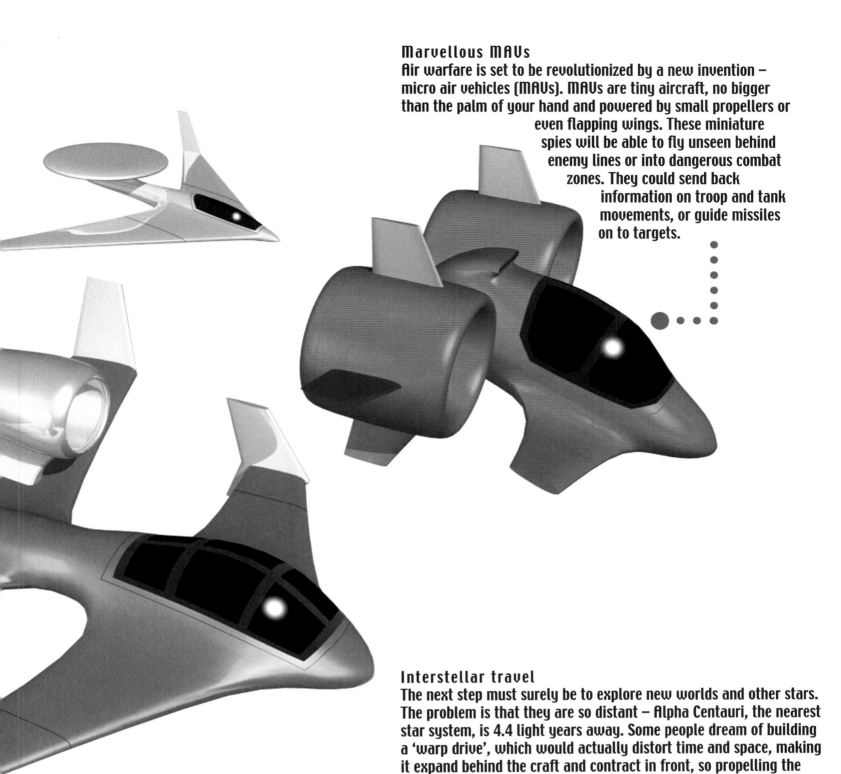

Marvellous MAVs

Air warfare is set to be revolutionized by a new invention – micro air vehicles (MAVs). MAVs are tiny aircraft, no bigger than the palm of your hand and powered by small propellers or even flapping wings. These miniature spies will be able to fly unseen behind enemy lines or into dangerous combat zones. They could send back information on troop and tank movements, or guide missiles on to targets.

Interstellar travel

The next step must surely be to explore new worlds and other stars. The problem is that they are so distant – Alpha Centauri, the nearest star system, is 4.4 light years away. Some people dream of building a 'warp drive', which would actually distort time and space, making it expand behind the craft and contract in front, so propelling the spacecraft to new parts of the Universe.

SPACE PLANES

One of the most exciting concepts on the horizon is the space plane, which would take off and land like a normal jet airliner, but fly round the Earth in space at more than Mach 26. With virtually no friction above the atmosphere to slow it down, it could cut journey times to the other side of the globe to less than two hours!

There are plans for space planes that could cut journey times to other parts of the world dramatically, a new breed of airship, robot fighters, and tiny micro-surveillance planes. There are also many possibilities that might become reality one day, such as gravity modulation – the idea of shielding an aircraft from gravity so that it weighs virtually nothing and can easily be launched into space. Whatever the future holds, it's bound to be astonishing!

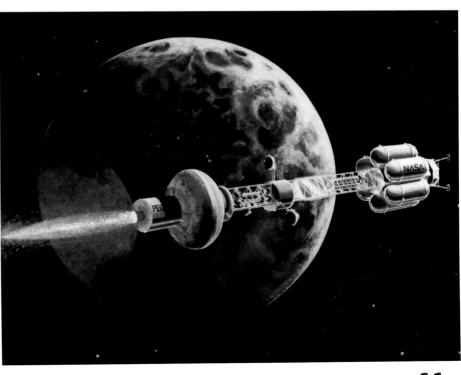

GLOSSARY

aerodynamic Shaped to travel well through the air.

aerofoil The cross-section shape of a wing, seen from the side, which produces lift when air flows over it. Propellers and rotor blades also have an aerofoil shape.

aileron A hinged surface attached to the trailing edge of an aeroplane's wing.

airbrake A flat, oblong control surface that emerges from a wing at right angles. Airbrakes extend to disturb the flow of air over the wings, decreasing lift and increasing drag.

altitude The height of an aircraft above the ground.

ballast A material carried during flight that can be thrown out to reduce the load and increase lift.

banking Turning in flight, with the airplane tilted so that one wing-tip is higher than the other one.

biplane An airplane with two sets of wings, positioned one above the other.

bulkhead A solid partition that separates one part of an airplane from another.

canopy The transparent covering to a cockpit, made of either toughened glass or plastic.

cockpit The compartment where a pilot or aircrew sits during flight.

control surface A movable surface on the tail or wing that changes the airflow over an airplane.

dorsal On the back of an aircraft.

drag A force acting on an aircraft that resists its forward movement through the air.

duralumin A strong lightweight metal made of aluminium mixed with copper, magnesium and sometimes silicon.

elevator A hinged control surface on an airplane's horizontal tail-plane.

elevon A combined elevator and aileron. Delta-winged airplanes such as Concorde have no tail-planes, so they have elevons on the rear edges of the wings.

fin The vertical part of an airplane's tail assembly. The fin gives stability and stops the rear of the plane swinging left or right.

flak Anti-aircraft fire.

flap A hinged surface attached to the trailing edge of the wing. Flaps slide back and down to increase lift at slow speeds, especially when taking off and landing.

flaperon A combined flap and aileron, consisting of a very long control surface along a plane's trailing wing edge.

former A vertical supporting frame inside an aircraft's fuselage that helps to give it shape.

fuselage The tubular body of an aircraft, to which the engines, rotors and wings are attached.

horsepower A measure of an engine's power.

hydraulic Powered by a pressurized liquid pumped through cables.

jet engine An engine that draws air in, burns fuel inside a combustion chamber, and then expels a jet of hot exhaust gases to provide thrust.

jettison To cast off or discard in flight.

jinking Moving with a rapidly changing left-to-right motion.

Hindenburg

lift The upwards force that raises an aircraft off the ground. Lift is generated by wings, rotor blades or lighter-than-air gases.

longeron The main horizontal strips in the frame of an aircraft's fuselage.

monoplane An airplane with one set of wings.

pitch The up-and-down movement of an airplane's nose, when the aircraft climbs or dives.

pressurized Kept at normal atmospheric pressure. Aircraft cabins are pressurized for high altitude flight so that crew and passengers can breathe normally, without the aid of oxygen masks.

pylon A projecting part of a wing or fuselage to which weapons or extra fuel tanks can be attached.

radar (Radio Detection And Ranging) A navigation and tracking system that sends out radio waves and detects the 'echoes' that bounce back off clouds, landscape features, aircraft and ships.

retractable Able to be withdrawn into the body of an aircraft.

roll The side-to-side movement of an airplane, in which the plane tilts so that one wing rises and the other falls.

rudder A hinged control surface attached to the tail fin. The rudder controls yaw, making the plane turn left or right.

skid A ski-like runner under an aircraft to support the craft on the ground or prevent damage when landing.

slat A control surface on the leading edge of the wing.

spar A main load-carrying support in the framework of a wing. Spars run along the length of the wing.

spoiler A panel built into the wing that can be raised to spoil or disrupt the flow of air over the wing, reducing lift and slowing the plane down.

sponson A float projecting from the side of an aircraft that gives it buoyancy and keeps it balanced in water.

tail-plane A horizontal, wing-like surface attached to the rear of an aircraft that stops the tail bobbing up and down.

thrust The force that pushes an aircraft forwards through the air.

triplane An airplane with three sets of wings, positioned one above the other.

turbine A set of angled, rotating blades that produces power from the energy of a stream of fluid, such as fast-moving air or engine exhaust gases.

turbofan A jet engine with a huge fan in front to suck more air into the engine and give extra power. Most of the air bypasses the combustion chamber and is expelled as a cold jet.

turbojet A jet engine that channels all of the air-intake through its combustion chamber, expelling it as a hot jet.

turboprop An engine in which compressed air and fuel are burnt and the hot waste gases used to turn a set of turbine blades. The turbine then drives a propeller.

turbulence The rough flow of air. Turbulence gives aircraft a bumpy flight.

undercarriage An aircraft's wheels and the struts that link them to the aircraft. The undercarriage supports the aircraft on the ground and during take-off.

ventral On the 'belly' or underside of an aircraft.

yaw The left-to-right movement of an airplane's nose, when the plane turns left or right.

INDEX